Also by Jerry Dennis

From a Wooden Canoe
Canoeing Michigan Rivers
It's Raining Frogs and Fishes
A Place on the Water
The Bird in the Waterfall

"Jerry Dennis is on his way to becoming a giant of classic outdoor literature."

—Vin Sparano, Editor Emeritus, *Outdoor Life*

"Here are some of the best stories about growing up in the outdoors since Hemingway wrote the Nick Adams stories."

—*Flint* (Michigan) *Journal*

"In this book, Dennis elevates the typical 'outdoor' essay, usually a mere recollection of adventures while hunting, fishing, camping, canoeing, or pursuing other outdoor activities. He has transcended the typical by blending in elements of 'nature' writing: observation, research, speculation about the world in which the sportsman places himself."

—*The Oakland Press*

"Jerry's style is comfortable and readable. I found myself laughing out loud at some of his situations and contemplating deeper meanings in others."

—*Midwest Fly Fishing*

"One hesitates to refer to Jerry Dennis as an 'outdoor' writer or *The River Home* as a book about 'fishing'; both have far transcended their respective genres. Dennis is an extraordinarily gifted writer, and these beautifully written essays and stories—warm, wise, and funny—use angling to explore the timeless themes of family, friendship, home, and a man's place in the natural world. Never cynical—even in the face of the loss and change that haunt all fishermen—always contemplative and celebratory, *The River Home* is a perfect gem."

—Jim Fergus, author of *A Hunter's Road*

"Early on in *The River Home*, Jerry Dennis makes a distinction between hearing and listening: 'We *hear* traffic and airport noise. We *listen* to laughing children and hooting doves; to wind-stirred aspen, trout sipping mayflies.' Well, listen up, Jerry Dennis writes words to listen to, and you won't want to miss one."

—Pete Fromm, author of *Dry Rain*
and *Indian Creek Chronicles*

"With a jeweler's eye and passionate voice, Jerry Dennis explores the woods and rivers he loves and makes us feel alive about *our* own special places. This is the magic of the book, how it reminds us how full of wonder a summer or winter day can be, if only we open our eyes. This is a book about fishing, yes—fishing, above all, for those wondrous places in your life. This is a book you'll want to pass along to friends."

—Doug Stanton, Contributing Editor, *Men's Journal*

"*The River Home* is a delightful book. In fact it is one of the most enjoyable fishing books that I have ever read. It's the kind of book you could read in one sitting: a sitting that would appropriately take place in a comfortable chair beside a fireplace in a rustic log cabin somewhere. At least this is the kind of mental image I get when reading Jerry Dennis's fine work."

—*The Riverwatch*

"Many times I stopped to reread passages simply because they were so well written—and that's about the highest praise I can give any writer."

—*Silent Sports*

"Collections of essays about the outdoors and fishing crowd the shelves, but Dennis's fresh writing and marvelous insights merit special attention. This fine collection will appeal to fans of Hal Borland, W. D. Wetherell, and Nick Lyons, as well as to those who enjoy the essays of fiction writers William Tapply and Thomas McGuane."

—*Booklist*

"Even if you've never pulled on a pair of waders, you should read this funny and wise book about fly fishing—and a lot more."

—*Georgia Times-Union*

"Whether you are a fisherman or not, the author's clear prose is compelling and a pleasure to read."

—*Chattanooga Free Press*

The River Home

An Angler's Explorations

JERRY DENNIS

Illustrations by Glenn Wolff

THOMAS DUNNE BOOKS
ST. MARTIN'S GRIFFIN
NEW YORK

THOMAS DUNNE BOOKS.
An imprint of St. Martin's Press.

Design by Ellen R. Sasahara

Library of Congress Cataloging-in-Publication Data

Dennis, Jerry.
The river home : an angler's explorations / Jerry Dennis ; illustrations by Glenn Wolff.
p. cm.
"Thomas Dunne Books."
ISBN 0-312-18594-4 (hc)
ISBN 0-312-25415-6 (pbk)
1. Fly fishing—Michigan—Anecdotes. 2. Dennis, Jerry.
I. Title.
SH509.D46 1998
799.1'24'09774—dc21 98-11958
CIP

First St. Martin's Griffin Edition: March 2000

10 9 8 7 6 5 4 3 2 1

For

DANIEL R. OLSON,

who loved the river

1979–1997

Contents

STORIES

Essays

Home Again

Home is where the heart is, and these days mine is sprawling all over the place. That's a result of having traveled a fair amount recently and having moved a few years ago from a small house in our city's central neighborhood, where my wife and sons and I lived for nearly a decade, to a farmhouse on a peninsula in Lake Michigan's Grand Traverse Bay. We moved just ten miles, but it seems much farther.

Not since we were children had my wife and I stayed in one place as long as we stayed on Eleventh Street. We lived through many of the usual turmoils and triumphs there: teaching the kids to walk and ride bicycles, patching sidewalk injuries, whipping up Halloween costumes and birthday parties and spontaneous neighborhood barbecues. It was a place that made friends feel they could arrive unannounced, carrying bags of groceries and bottles of wine, and stay up so late cooking, eating, talking, and playing music that they had no choice but to stay over and sleep on the couch. We planted gardens there and supplied sunflower seeds to several generations of birds and squirrels. We watched neighbors move in and move out and witnessed marriages, divorces, births, and funerals. We played baseball in the street with the neighborhood kids and retrieved their Frisbees from our roof. We made friends with the mailman.

In that small house on its seventy-five-foot lot we learned about the richness that comes from living for a long time in one place. It's a lesson our grandparents could have taught us if we had stayed still long enough to listen. Our generation and our parents' generation have been restless, changing houses and communities as casually as we change automobiles, yet those of us who stay in one spot for even a few years are surprised to learn that with time every tree and flower garden in the yard—and every creek, pond, playground, and basketball court in the neighborhood—accumulates memories. Spend enough time in a place, and your experiences there grow layered and complex, which is one way to build a fuller life. Putting down roots can tap into deep sources of nourishment.

Exploring new terrain, on the other hand, strips us free of old notions and helps us see the world with fresh eyes. Most of my childhood was spent twenty miles from our new house, and Gail and I lived half that distance away during our years on Eleventh Street, yet Old Mission Peninsula is wonderfully free of associations for us. We moved here with the enthusiasm we would have carried on a move across the continent, or even to a different continent. We stepped inside this 125-year-old farmhouse with its second-floor dormers and sagging floors and eminently sensible Cape Cod design—the long sloping rear of the house backed protectively against the north wind—and it was like stepping into a new life. A new house, new neighbors, new places to explore: We had no idea what to expect, and it thrilled us.

One bright January day soon after our move, I spent the afternoon following a red fox as it meandered across the snow-covered fields near the house. I stayed a hundred yards back, downwind, and the fox never saw me. It stopped now and then to investigate clumps of underbrush for voles and field mice, to lift a leg and mark territory, to sit and scratch itself and look around idly like a domestic dog. It's tempting to say that a city dweller would never see such a thing. But I know better. In Traverse City our maple-lined street and backyard, with its box elders and lilacs, were home to raccoons, skunks, squirrels, hares, and opossums. We were a short walk from the wetlands and woods bordering the grounds of the defunct state hospital across Division Street, and just five blocks from the Boardman River, where my sons and I fished in the summer for resident bass and pike and in the spring and fall for steelhead, brown trout, and salmon. Gail and I stood with the boys at night in the yard to watch the aurora borealis and wrapped ourselves in blankets on the grass and counted meteors during the Perseid shower. One week the four of us gathered in the alley every evening after sunset and watched the tight triangular massing of Venus, Jupiter, and Mars, a conjunction not due to appear again for 120 years. Feeders hanging in our backyard attracted dozens of species of songbirds. A few blocks from our house a friend watched a plummeting hawk strike a pigeon in flight, then follow it to the ground, hood it with its wings, and tear its breast apart. I once flushed a sharp-tailed grouse—a rare bird in our part of Michigan—from the sidewalk in front of the Salvation Army store at the end of our block and watched it soar up Maple Street toward the playground behind the elementary school. That same fall a bald eagle lingered for days near Clinch Park in downtown Traverse City, and a motorist struck and killed a young black bear on a busy stretch of highway between our city's two malls. Nature does not recognize city-limit signs.

But of course nature is more prominent in the country, and much easier to observe. We saw stars in the city, but only the brightest of them. Now we witness the full breadth of the Milky Way and can sense that all the space between the brightest stars is occupied by lesser ones. During meteor showers we see not just the largest and most spectacular meteors but also the brief flashes made by particles the size of birdseed.

Not that we live in isolation. We have neighbors within shouting distance, and too many cars passing on Blue Water Road, and a subdivision growing noisily in the field across the road. Our single acre of land is all that remains of an eighty-acre cherry orchard that once covered both sides of the road nearly to the bay. Like many of the orchards on the peninsula, this one was uprooted years ago and the land parceled for development. But our acre of lawn and gardens is shaded by grandfather maples and screened by a fencerow of cedars along the road. It gives us enough privacy for now, and we like the neighbors very much.

After we moved to the peninsula our first urge was to get to know the waters of the bay and the few small ponds nearby. The only way to become acquainted with a river or lake is to embrace it: Walk the shores, wade the shallows, cast a line into it, paddle a canoe on it, rig up a rope swing and drop, shouting, into the heart of it. Knowledge comes with experience, a word whose root translates into "being in peril." Risking peril puts us closer to a place than we can ever get by standing at a safe distance, watching. We need to risk sunburn and wet feet, mild hypothermia, sore muscles, blistered hands, loneliness, and humiliation before we can know a place well enough to feel at home in it. In Traverse City I felt at home on the Boardman River and the portion of Kid's Creek that flows from the state hospital downstream through town to the river. On Old Mission I'm at home now within a few square miles of hardwoods and cherry orchards and along the shoreline surrounding them. Early on July mornings I can walk from my house to East Bay, wade among reeds and rocks along shore, and cast deerhair flies for smallmouth bass. On this water, famed throughout the world for its fishing, I'm often the only human in sight.

When I built houses for a living, I liked the work of measuring, cutting, and nailing, and I found it satisfying to step back at the end of each day to see what I had accomplished. But I never believed I was building homes. That takes time, life, and love, not the work of carpenters. For a house to become a home it has to be lived in. The walls have to become saturated with cooking smells and candle smoke, the floors have to be anointed with spilled milk and tears and mud dried in the shape of tennis-shoe treads. There must be smudges on the windows, pennies in the furnace vents, dog hair on the carpet, a smear of toothpaste in the sink. The space inside needs to be filled for years with voices, music, and laughter. A house, no matter how skillfully built, is not finished until it has been cured in ten thousand ordinary moments.

My brother and I and, later, our adopted sister grew up in a house surrounded by so many lakes, woods, and fields that our early years had the feel of an extended weekend in the country. Home to us was the house, our yard, the forty acres of hardwoods across the road, and, of course, especially, the lake. Rick and I could handle oars and outboard motors almost before we could ride bicycles. Melissa spent her early childhood in inner-city Louisville, but when she came to Long Lake with my parents at age thirteen, she took to the water with the natural grace of an aquatic mammal. She was always the first in the lake every spring, wading out and diving under in April, when the water was only two or three weeks past frozen and so cold it flushed her skin and made her hoot in agony and delight. From then until the cold returned in autumn, she was more often in the water than out of it. During the summers none of us wanted to travel. We wanted to stay home. Our definition of the word included perhaps a square mile of land and water, and for a long time that was enough.

But our homes tend to expand as we grow older. They expand to include larger circles of friends and the places where we go to work, play, and relax. They expand to include the rivers and lakes where we fish and boat, the woods where we hunt and hike, every place that has emotional and historical significance for us. The larger our territory and the more we care about it, the greater our outrage when it is stolen or dumped on. "Not in my backyard" is a familiar cry of people refusing to allow uncontrolled development or the disposal of wastes in the vicinity of their homes. It expresses a literal sentiment. A backyard can stretch for miles and miles; a home can be as big as a continent or a planet.

My backyard now includes about a dozen counties in northern Michigan. It's rolling country, tilled a hundred centuries ago by glaciers and since grown up with hardwoods and conifers, where cedar swamps surround meadows of bracken and goldenrod, and stands of jackpine and aspen divide plains dotted by the weathered gray stumps of pines that were cut a hundred years ago and have never grown back. You can't go far in any direction without descending to water. It's land spilling over with lakes and ponds, crossed by rivers, and bounded on all sides by the Great Lakes.

Scattered among those shorelines, fields, and woods are the remains of old homesteads. Often all that is seen of them is a thicket of lilacs and a few gnarled apple trees near a sunken foundation, with maybe an ancient barn falling slowly into itself. After the Civil War a surge of settlers arrived in northern Michigan to take advantage of the Homestead Act of 1862, which for a nominal fee gave each family up to 160 acres of cut-over forest. Many of the settlers were determined enough to dig out the stumps and make pastures and fields, but few were determined enough to stay on when the land proved so infertile that it could scarcely support a crop.

To live here even today requires determination. The northern half of the state contains a remarkable density of jacks-of-all-trades. We work as carpenters, bricklayers, timber cutters, waitresses, auto mechanics, and convenience-store clerks—sometimes all in the same year. We plant forty acres of sandy soil with pine seedlings and harvest them seven years later for Christmas trees. We hunt and fish for subsistence as much as for recreation. We sell crafts to tourists. We work in tiny machine shops building parts for the automobile plants in Detroit and Flint.

A few of us manage to live off the land, either by farming or from gas and oil royalties earned by the wells bobbing in the pasture out back. Some pockets of fertile soil are farmed for corn and potatoes. Orchards and vineyards thrive where the climate is kept moderate along the Lake Michigan shore, but they are dwindling in size and number as farmers and wine makers realize that their profits will never equal the offers of developers eager to convert acreage into subdivisions.

It can be difficult to find natives. Our numbers swell as people from southern Michigan retire or get laid off or just chuck it all and head north. Most move here because of the rivers, lakes, and woods but find that the lovely country and the clean air come with a price. Good jobs are scarce and pay is low. You can find Ph.D.s managing sporting-goods stores, architects building houses, former auto executives throwing pottery in barnwood-sided studios. We have rural pockets as impoverished as the worst of Appalachia: You can meet men who haven't worked a steady job in ten years; their families might get by on food stamps and poached venison, but the old man finds a way to buy a new 4X4 pickup every three years.

LIKE MOST OF the United States and Canada, the history of northern Michigan can be written around the twin themes of abundance and waste. Once it was land overflowing with riches, from beaver pelts to white pine, from copper to iron ore, from passenger pigeons to whitefish, lake trout, and sturgeon. The first white entrepreneurs considered it a storehouse of unlimited wealth and insisted to anyone who would listen that the beaver, pines, copper, and fish were inexhaustible. Even the most sober-minded observers estimated that it would take hundreds of years to cut the last of the enormous white and red pines growing in lush thickets across northern Michigan, by which time a new crop would have matured in their place. Instead the forests were decimated within a few decades, and except for tiny patches of virgin pine near Grayling and on the Keweenaw Peninsula, the stands of giant trees are gone.

Exploitation continues today and is still justified with soothing words. State forests have been carved into precise rectangles of an acre or two, one every half mile in some places. At the center of each clear-cut is a large green pump, its horse head nodding hypnotically as it sucks oil from deposits left when the land was covered by ocean. New roads have been cut to access the wells; two-track tote roads used by loggers and horse-drawn wagons a century ago have been widened into gravel highways big enough to accommodate trucks pulling heavy machinery. When the wells are dry and the pumps are pulled, the roads will remain, kept perpetually rutted by hunters, fishermen, mushroom hunters, woodcutters. In the woods, along the logging trails, you can find abandoned cars, home appliances shot through with bullet holes, entire living-room suites leaking white stuffing. Along the county roads are neat-as-a-pin ranch houses next door to trailers set on blocks and surrounded by three wrecked cars, a radio-dish antenna, a dog kennel, and a snowmobile that squats all summer on the lawn—and a mile away is a nationally promoted resort complex with a ski slope, a sixty-four-hole golf course designed by Arnold Palmer, and rows of condominiums jutting above the tree line like vertebrae.

I've lived most of my life in this complex place and feel at home here, but I don't know what it means to love the land. I suspect I'm incapable of the deep connection felt by my grandfather, who owned a cherry farm and maple-syrup business in Leelanau County and worked season after season in his woods, cornfields, and orchards. We seem, as a people, to be losing our sense of rootedness. Maybe we lost it when we stopped working the land. Maybe our sweat and tears have to mingle with the bones of our ancestors before we can feel deeply connected to a place.

In our time caring about a place means watching it change. It isn't easy. Old men go around in pissy moods because the world refuses to stay the way it was. They're angry because suddenly everyone has a personal computer and a cellular phone and nobody consulted them first; because there's too much traffic and it moves too fast; because the woods where they've hunted all their lives have been divided into lots, and the lakes where they've fished all their lives have been taken over by water-skiers and personal watercraft. The world has been altered beyond recognition, and mostly in the last few years. Such rapid change can induce a landed, psychological version of diver's bends. The psyche, unable to adapt, becomes poisoned and bent with pain. One symptom is a tendency to bellow at the TV; another, irritation with strangers.

Not far from where I live is a section of trout river that Kelly Galloup and I have fished a dozen times in the last couple years. It's water overlooked by most of the fly-fishers who congregate in the better-known sections upstream. We've caught relatively few trout there, but they've been bigger than average. One day when Kelly, Pat Moore, and I pulled into the access site to launch Kelly's drift boat, another fisherman was already there. He was not happy to see us. He stomped around his boat, throwing gear inside. Finally he could not contain his anger.

"Why are you fishing here?" he demanded. "Why do you

guys from Traverse City have to come over and ruin it? I've lived here all my life, and I've fished this river since I was a kid, and now I have to watch you bastards ruin the fishing just like you ruined the partridge hunting."

This outburst took place at a public-access site on a river thirty miles from where Kelly and I grew up. Between us we've fished the river more than fifty years. We consider the upper river *ours.* In the last two seasons while floating this particular stretch, we had seen only two other anglers. We were not even sharing water with the man—he was going upstream, we were going down. It was easy to dismiss him as a jerk. He was being ignorant, irrational, obnoxious. But we saw his point.

We're afraid of losing what we don't even own. It's pure selfishness. We want fifteen miles of prime trout river completely to ourselves. We want a lake of our own. We want to chase away every fisherman and water-skier, bulldoze the cottages, build bonfires of docks and ice shanties. We want to post the property every hundred feet with no-trespassing signs and patrol it on horseback. We want to dump truckloads of trout in the water, as if they were seeds thrown into our private garden, and harvest them for winter. A length of river, a wooded hilltop, a stretch of public shoreline should be enough for anyone. But they're not. Too many people are building too many houses and moving into the spaces we once considered ours. It's an old story, not that that makes it easier. On the contrary.

I'm convinced that the human heart can expand to fill all available space. Moving and travel enlarge those spaces, landing us in new, strange places while we're still under the spell of the familiar ones, and teaching us unexpected things about ourselves and the world. It makes coming home a revelation. I might not care for the land the way my grandfather did, but I care for it nonetheless. When I am gone for long, and especially when I visit places without clear lakes and rivers, my homing urge grows strong. Even where the fishing and the scenery are extraordinary, I soon miss the wooded hills and the dunes and the cedar-scented, sand-and-gravel rivers of northern Michigan. If my feelings for this place are contradictory, that's not unusual. And if it does not quite satisfy my needs and expectations, that's not unusual either.

I like our home in the country, but it surprises me to discover how much I miss walking on maple-covered sidewalks to the Sixth Street library and playing basketball in the alley with my sons and their friends. Growing up a country kid, I assumed I would always remain one, so I was not prepared to find myself drawn to cities. After traveling in spacious Iceland I was so happy to be in New York that I walked for blocks down crowded avenues and elbowed into the busiest Irish bar I could find. It was filled with animated and colorful people, each more fascinating by far than the volcanoes, glaciers, and rivers I had just explored. The world grows smaller as we grow older, but it is not a small world. It widens, in fact, to accommodate our interests.

As an undergraduate at the University of Louisville, I sat in a packed auditorium listening to an address by the late Argentine-born poet and story writer Jorge Luis Borges. He was past eighty then, frail and blind, yet he stood unaided on the stage and spoke of life and literature with such passion that tremors ran up my spine. At one point, in response to a question from the audience, Borges corrected an assumption about his citizenship. "I am not an Argentine," he said. "Like Socrates, I am a citizen of the world."

Few of us have the capacity to embrace the entire world, but it seems a worthy aspiration. When I lose heart or feel constricted and cut off from world events, I walk the fields and woods of my home and climb hills above cherry orchards to stand in a Lake Michigan wind that carries the scents of fresh water, tallgrass prairies, Rocky Mountain snowfields, and Pacific surf. It is the same wind that surges across the treeless plateaus of Iceland and North Dakota, that funnels through the gorges of the Andes, that swirls down Twenty-third Street near Lexington and lifts the pages of used paperbacks lined up for sale on the sidewalk.

The idea of one wind, one world, is new to me. I passed the decade of my twenties in motion, living no place for long, convinced that I belonged nowhere in particular. Now, beginning my forties, I find it strange and heartening to feel at home on the earth at last.

Why Fish?

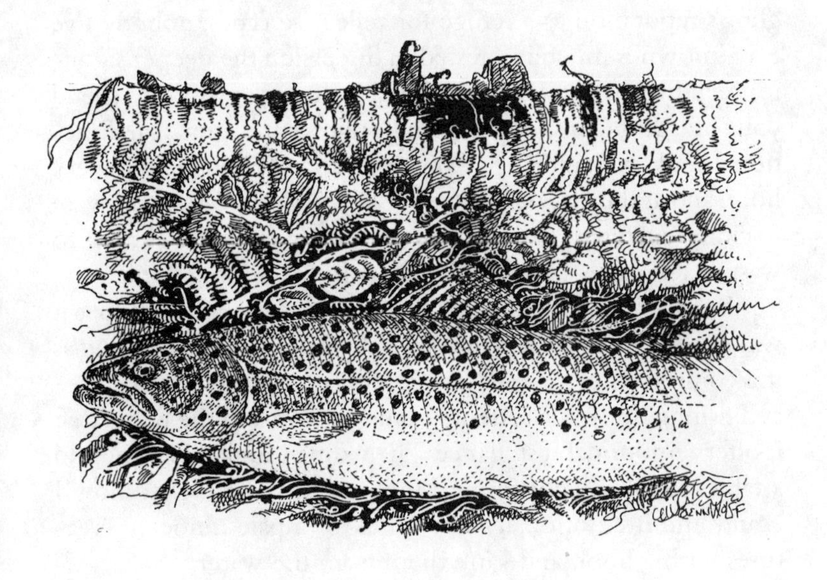

One evening I had dinner at a restaurant with people I hardly knew, and in the course of conversation a smiling woman in an evening gown and diamond jewelry asked why I fished. I didn't know quite what to say. I had given the question much thought over the years but had never come up with a good answer. Fishing is a simple pleasure, after all, and simple pleasures don't hold up well to scrutiny. Under examination it can appear ridiculous. It can become a parody of ancient hunting-gathering behavior, a residue of instincts made meaningless by modern life. It begins to appear pointless, frivolous, even cruel. And if you prefer not to kill what you catch, the only practical justification for the sport is made moot every time you release a fish.

Naturally such thinking drains the fun away. In spite of angling's reputation as a refuge for reflective types, nobody I've ever known is much interested in discussing the deeper significance of the sport. It comes down to how you want to spend your life. You can spend it doing only what is practical, functional, and profitable—making yourself accountable for every hour, and at the end of the day tallying your time as if you were stacking currency. Or you can be a bit wasteful. I choose to waste a few hours. More than a few hours. Enough said.

But the woman required an answer, so I explained that it was important to understand the difference between fishing as it is commonly perceived—as goofing off, a way to kill time—and fishing done with attention and passion and the belief that it offers emotional sustenance. The woman smiled as if she had a tablespoon of paint thinner in her mouth and asked how I could find it emotionally sustaining to impale innocent creatures with a hook and yank them from the water.

There was a silence—one of many that evening—and the people at the table looked intently at their plates. I tried to lighten the mood by joking about my luck as an angler. Most days, after all, I impale very few creatures, innocent or otherwise. But the woman was not amused. I suggested that in a world as troubled as ours, fishing is among the least harmful of activities. Speaking in a voice that began in a normal tone but ended in a howl, she said that she did not consider brutality a harmless activity. There was another silence, longer than the first, and finally the host steered the conversation in a different direction, and that was the end of it.

The incident bothered me, and I was sorry I did not have a better answer for the woman. It nagged for a few days; then I forgot it.

• • •

THAT SUMMER MY son and I got lost while canoeing in Michigan's Upper Peninsula. Not lost exactly: turned around. Not even turned around, to be honest, since we were portaging a trail in a three-by-three-mile tract of forest and lakes bordered on three sides by gravel roads and on the fourth by an abandoned railroad grade. If we had examined a county map we would have known exactly where we were. But we did not have a map: That was the point. On a wooded ridge, where the trail idled beneath an emerald canopy of maples, I leaned the canoe against the crotch of a tree and stepped from beneath it to rest.

"Looks like we're lost now," I said.

"Goody," Aaron said, and grinned.

He was eleven years old and hungry for adventure. He wanted to travel to places he had never been, get face to face with wild country, catch enough fish and gather enough berries to create the illusion that we were surviving by our wits. This was not deep wilderness, but he didn't know that. To him it was as wild as Borneo.

Resting beside the portage trail, I mentioned that the woods and the view of water through the trees reminded me of a place I had visited once in Quebec. For a moment there was disappointment on my son's face, and I was sorry I had said anything. He did not want our experience muddied by memories of my previous experiences. He wanted this to stand by itself. And of course he was right.

No place is like any other place. When I looked closer I saw that the hardwoods were not pure, that the maples were mixed with hemlock and spruce and, farther down the trail, smoke-colored tamaracks with foliage soft as feathers, all growing above an understory of sweet fern and thimbleberries. Then I saw the sky, that brittle turquoise that looks like no other sky I have ever seen. We were pretending to be lost somewhere south of Munising in a region that was so unmistakably the Upper Peninsula that I wondered how I could even have *thought* of another place.

We had established a camp on a pine-masted island in the middle of the largest lake in the area and had three days to explore and fish. We fished the big lake's bays and drop-offs and portaged the canoe over trails that linked a network of about twenty small lakes. On the first day we saw two parties of canoeists, both on their way out. After that we had about 5,500 acres to ourselves.

Success is important when you fish with children. Aaron was not content to spend his time fruitlessly. He wanted action. While I cast poppers and streamers with a fly rod, he cast jigs and twisters with his spinning rod, a combination so lethal it should be included in military survival kits. Every tenth cast or so he caught a largemouth or smallmouth bass, a bluegill, a perch, or a northern pike. None of them was very large.

Aaron's passion for fishing comes and goes. Usually it is far down on his list of interests, but occasionally he gives himself to it completely. On a creek not far from home, we once spent a day pursuing small trout. Brookies and rainbows were about evenly mixed, and that day they were more ravenous than usual. Aaron discovered that if he was quiet and moved slowly, he could catch a trout every time he lowered his bait into the base of a tiny falls or the dark pool beneath a log. He caught trout one after another and wanted to keep every one. To avoid a massacre I enlarged the legal size and convinced him that most of those he caught were too small to keep. Once he paused in his fishing and said, "Listen. I hear music." I heard it too, the music of brook water trickling over stones and plunging over ledges. Then he was fishing again, crawling on his knees, lowering his bait with absolute concentration into the creek. He seemed to grow more feral every moment.

Our canoe trip in the Upper Peninsula awakened that feral self. The more he fished, the more he wanted to fish. The farther we went on portage trails and unfamiliar lakes, the farther he wanted to go. We paddled, portaged, and fished so many hours each day that it was dark by the time we returned to our camp on the island. We would build a fire and cook something simple and fast, then eat in silence. The nights were clear, with so much starlight reflecting off the lake that we could see the bull's-eye rings of feeding fish. At midnight, after being on the water fourteen hours and so weary that he was nearly incoherent, my son wanted to go out on the lake and cast.

One morning, while Aaron sat in the bow scanning the water, I nosed the canoe through a thick fringe of lily pads surrounding the shore of the big lake. Suddenly Aaron raised his hand for us to stop. A rod's length away, facing shore and hovering just above bottom in two feet of water, was a muskie. It was as long as a canoe paddle.

I assumed that something was wrong with the fish. I once discovered a five-pound brown trout finning in a half foot of water along the edge of a river. Only after I had cast to it for twenty minutes did I stalk close enough to see that it had been blinded in both eyes.

It seemed likely that the muskie was similarly disabled. Aaron wanted to try to catch it, but I was skeptical. Whispering my doubts, I reached for the spinning rod and tied on a rubber frog, our only weedless lure.

I handed the rod to Aaron, and he lowered the lure in front of the muskie. The frog was dressed with a pair of flexible rubber legs that spun like propellers when it moved. The muskie turned slightly. It flared its gills, shot forward, and swallowed the thing.

Aaron was too quick: He pulled the lure away. There was a swirl of water and silt, and the muskie disappeared.

I suggested we move on; Aaron wanted to wait. His optimism was charming, but I knew better. I've made too many casts to fish that would not strike, and spent too many hours waiting for fish that would not return. The muskie was rocketing toward the middle of the lake, where it would spend the next two weeks in seclusion. I was sure we would never see it again.

We beached the canoe and walked the shoreline, looking for other fish. Half an hour later we returned to the canoe, pushed out into the lily pads, and found the muskie—or one just like it—finning on the bottom as before. Again it faced shore, its eyes focused on the surface.

Sometimes I'm slow on the uptake. The muskie was in the shallows feeding on frogs—what else?—and by chance I had selected the one lure it might attack without hesitation.

Aaron insisted it was my turn. I flipped the frog into an opening in the lily pads a few feet in front of the fish. The lure, legs whirling, settled to the bottom. I gave it a twitch that caused it to burrow, sending up a little cloud of silt. The muskie froze for a moment, as if it could not believe its good fortune, then pounced.

If I had been thinking clearly I would have set the hook with a sidearm motion, keeping the rod low to the water, seating the hook in the corner of the muskie's mouth. But I was too surprised to think clearly. I struck straight up, the way you would if you were fishing a vertical jig beneath your boat. The lure's single hook failed to penetrate. It held for a moment, just long enough for the water to churn with mud as the muskie rolled like a gigged alligator. Then it was off. This time it did not return.

We saw no other muskies that trip. Aaron caught many bass up to sixteen inches long, and a dozen northerns about legal size, and one evening I hooked a three-pound largemouth that slammed a popper and jumped in classic, headshaking fashion. Our last day, while we drifted with the breeze over a gravel point on the big lake, Aaron hooked something that ran line off his reel, tangled deep in weeds on the bottom, and broke off before we could see it.

That night we sat up after dinner tending the fire. At some point, late, I stirred the coals with a stick and watched sparks spiral into the sky.

"Look," I said.

Just above the trees to the north were lights. They looked at first like beams from distant spotlights searching the sky, but as we watched they grew brighter and began to climb. They climbed slowly, always in motion, spouting and falling like fountains, swaying like silk curtains in a breeze. They climbed until they reached the top of the sky and began to spread rays of light in all directions from a center almost straight above us. Then the rays changed colors, blending slowly from white to pink, then from pink to green and blue, like wide swipes of luminous watercolors drifting across the stars.

Aaron had never seen an aurora that could match it. He watched until the colors faded and the shafts of light retreated toward the horizon. By then he could no longer keep his eyes open. I walked him into the tent and helped him into his sleeping bag.

While he slept I sat by the fire and thought about the events of the last three days. During the aurora display Aaron's face had opened until it seemed to give off light of its own. I had seen him shine with similar light during other moments—while we rested under the maples on the portage trail; while we stirred sparks from the campfire; while the muskie finned in the shallows beneath the lily pads. I thought how remarkable it was that I could remember countless equally vivid moments on lakes and rivers and in the woods, but only a few that took place indoors. It occurred to me that indoors we are not only insulated from the cold and shielded from the wind, we are cut off from experiencing the world. If Aaron grew up to remember these three days it would be because they had demanded effort and imposed risk and forced him to step away from the security of his everyday, indoor life. And then I knew what I should have said to the woman in the restaurant back home.

If I had had the wit and the woman had been inclined to listen, I could have told her that fishing makes us alert, pulls us out of our thoughts, and engages us in something bigger than ourselves. It's a restorative that cleanses us when we've become muddied and makes us healthy when we've become sickened. It's a brace against pessimism.

Fishing, I should have explained, teaches us to perform small acts with care. It humbles us. It enriches our friendships. It cultivates reverence for wild things and beautiful places. It reminds us that time needs occasionally to be squandered. It offers relief from overdue bills and endless chores and appalling world events. It makes us participants in nature instead of spectators, a crucial distinction because participants tend to become passionate and protective and spectators tend to become indifferent.

I could have said that looking down into a lake, an ocean, or a river is like looking up into the night sky, that both water and sky are filled with mysteries, and when we stare deeply into them we connect with every man and woman who has ever sensed the tugging vitality of the universe. We become part of a larger community, united by mysteries so vast that they make our differences of opinion and philosophy seem very small.

Anglers are people who want to get beneath the surface of things. I wish I could have made the woman at the dinner understand that fishing is simply a way to open our hearts to the world.

Fishing Buddies

When I was younger and more reckless, I would go fishing with anyone who asked. But I wised up fast the afternoon I stepped into a canoe with the man I'll call Adolph.

He had phoned out of the blue one evening and said that he had been fishing most of his life on a river he heard I was interested in. He offered to show me where all the big trout lived. I asked how big. He said real big. I said name a date.

We met near his home, in a bar with a few tables and chairs, a pool table, walls decorated with plastic beer promotions. Three or four guys sat at the bar looking straight ahead at nothing. One of them was Adolph. He was fortyish, big in the belly, dressed in faded green work clothes. We drank a couple of beers while he told me his life story; then we headed for the river.

We'd been on the water maybe fifteen minutes, just long enough to put a few bends behind us, when Adolph laid his paddle across the gunwales and narrated a long anecdote about a trip to Florida, whose highlight occurred when he was bass fishing on an inland lake and was attacked by a boatload of African-American revolutionaries who would certainly have killed him if he hadn't defended himself by firing volleys with a flare gun. He explained that he had been targeted for years by minority radicals and was a victim of constant harassment by the CIA, environmental activists, a former wife and her new husband, a crooked sheriff, the antihunting lobby, and his local chamber of commerce—all of them trying to drive him away simply because he had the courage to be a true-blue American. He hinted that there had been several attempts on his life before the one while bassin' in Florida.

When I was already quite uncomfortable, he pulled a small black revolver from the pocket of his trousers. A .38, I think. He aimed into the underbrush on the riverbank, cocked, and fired. The retort was sudden and flat, like slamming a cupped hand over your ear. He twisted around in the bow seat and winked at me. "Keeps her rust free," he said.

I wanted to get out of the canoe, but I didn't dare offend him. "I'd sure feel better if you put the gun away."

"Why?" he asked, his eyes going reptilian.

"The element of surprise. It's better if they don't know you're armed."

He grinned. He liked that. He put the gun in his pocket.

For the next two hours he presented me with his views on the supremacy of the white race, the evils of homosexuality, the secret sources of corruption in the government, and the need to eradicate all lily-livered liberals, abortionists, and women's rights advocates. He informed me that environmentalists were communist infiltrators sent to undermine our nation's industrial and economic foundations, that illegal immigrants should be shot as they scampered across our sacred borders, that U.S. foreign policy needed to be beefed up with a few judiciously placed nuclear blasts, and that guys like us were the only real hope for the future of what was left of the late, great U.S. of A.

All this was delivered in loud tones, with constant waving of his arms for emphasis, interrupted only by pauses to take long gulping drinks from the cans of beer he had brought in his cooler. He refrained from throwing the empties into the river—mentioning the fact proudly, as if he'd invented the concept—and insisted almost at gunpoint that I join him in drinking.

I didn't. I paddled. I paddled steadily and hard. When we passed two girls sunbathing on a private dock, Adolph shouted, "Hey, Baby! Whoo-whoo!" and I put my head down and concentrated on a racer's cadence: sixty strokes per minute, switch sides every six strokes, *hut!*

The trip ended without bloodshed and without either of us making a single cast into the river. We loaded the canoe onto Adolph's truck and drove back upstream to the put-in. He invited me to join him for dinner—"American food, none of that foreign pansy crap"—but I pleaded family obligations and ran for my car.

It was a good lesson. I learned to be more discriminating. And I believe that I'm now qualified to say what makes a good fishing buddy.

A good buddy is someone like Tom Carney, with whom I've spent ten years hunting grouse and woodcock and a few quality hours chasing trout. Tom and I once hiked into a small trout lake, set up camp under the pines along shore, and spent the evening fishing for rainbows that were cruising the drop-off, feeding on hatching midges. When it got dark we built a campfire and stayed up late talking. Then we crawled into our sleeping bags and slept.

In the night I came down with a fever. I had felt a bit lightheaded earlier, but thought it was because the fishing was so good and we hadn't taken time to eat. But I woke in the middle of the night and knew something was wrong. One moment I was shivering with cold, and the next I was so hot the perspiration spurted from me. By dawn, when Tom stirred awake, my sleeping bag was drenched. I ached in every muscle. I croaked the words "water" and "food," and Tom got up immediately to build a fire and start breakfast. But when he saw the lake churning with hundreds of feeding trout, he leaned back into the tent, tossed a nearly empty canteen and a box of blueberry Pop-Tarts on the ground next to me, and disappeared. I didn't see him again for three hours.

A good fishing buddy has his priorities straight.

Of all the guys I fish with, none has his priorities straighter than Kelly Galloup. Besides being a fly-shop owner, fishing guide, fly tier, taxidermist, bodybuilder, kick-boxer, champion downhill skier, former seminary student, and dedicated family man, he's an inspired and inspiring angler and one of the few people I've ever met who fishes with more passion than me. He's also one of the most opinionated, outspoken, direct, foulmouthed, quick-witted, clearheaded, honest, funny, infuriating, and altogether delightful people I know. Count on it: He always speaks his mind. Once I asked him what it was like to fish for steelhead in British Columbia. For the sake of the kids, here's the PG-13 version of what he said:

"It's the most incredible thing you'll ever do. It's way better than sex. You watch a beeping twenty-pound steelhead eat the beeping dry fly you're skating across the beeping Camp Pool on the Dean, and I guarantee you'll never be the same. I swear to God. People talk about the way having children changes their lives, but that's nothing. A steelhead comes blasting out of the water from five or six feet deep to chase the fly, and it's coming so hard it can't stop, its momentum launches it right into the air like it's been catapulted out of the water, and you realize this son of a bitch is *pissed,* there's no other word for it, and you don't know what it is you've done exactly, but somehow you have really pissed him off. You can see him coming from fifteen feet away, and you think there's no way he's going to miss that fly streaking by on the current at twenty miles per hour—after all, when's the last time you missed your face with a cheeseburger?—and you get a whole beeping body rush. There's nothing like it in the world. But he's so stoked up he overshoots the fly, vaults right over the top of it, and crashes into the river. It's like hand grenades going off. I watched one steelhead rise like that to my buddy Mike's fly eleven times in a row before it was finally hooked and landed. It came to the beeping fly three times on the same beeping cast, each time Mike going, 'Whoa! Beep! Did you see that?' and turning to see if I had seen it, and at that moment having the fish rise, boom! beep! and take it again, yanking line out in a screaming, ripping run, ten or twenty yards gone in a heartbeat, only to get off again. Three times on one cast! Listen: It changes your whole beeping life."

A good fishing buddy is entertaining.

Glenn Wolff, a relative newcomer to fishing, is entertaining in other ways. It was my privilege to accompany Glenn on his first attempt to fish the Hex hatch—the giant *Hexagenia* mayflies that provide the best opportunity in Michigan to hook big trout on dry flies. That night there was a good hatch and quite a few active fish, and Glenn, being generally patient and coolheaded, spent the entire evening casting to a single fish. He never raised the trout, but neither did he spook it. It turned out there was a good reason for that. There is no way of knowing how long he was casting blanks, but late in the hatch his tip section separated from his rod, slid the length of his line, and, without a fly to stop it, disappeared downstream. We couldn't find the tip section that night, but Glenn went back the next morning and found it floating on the lee side of an island. A few days later he was fishing the same water and when he was done for the day laid his rod on the top of his station wagon and left it there. He drove thirty miles home, and only when he was unloading his gear did he realize what he had done. He retraced his route and found the rod, undamaged, on the shoulder of one of the busiest highways around here. A week later he was walking away from the river and dropped his tip section in the swamp. That time he lost it for good.

Sometimes Glenn's adventures can be a little baffling. He called one day and asked in a sort of embarrassed, sidelong way if I had ever heard of a beaver taking a dry fly. He said he was fishing on the Platte above the hatchery and hooked something so big that it ran him into the backing and finally broke off. I asked if it was a fish, and he said he wasn't sure. It was either a very big fish or a medium-size beaver. I asked if it had fur, and he said he didn't know but it was dark and sleek looking. I asked if it had a tail, and he said yes, definitely. I asked if it was a fishy tail or a beavery tail, and he said it looked fishy but it was so big he thought it might be beavery. I said I suspected that he'd snagged a coho salmon that had slipped through the weir and was hiding out, waiting to spawn and die. He said he didn't think he snagged whatever it was because he clearly saw it suck his dry fly down, which is why he wondered if I had ever seen a beaver do that. I suggested that he had hooked one of the large brown trout that live in that section of the river. He said he didn't know, but if it was a trout it must have weighed about forty pounds, which on reflection seemed unlikely to both of us. In the end I had no idea what to think. I didn't have a clue.

A good fishing buddy keeps you guessing.

Doug Stanton is one of my literary pals. We call each other on the phone every few days and say things like, "I'll swap you five hundred words of wacky for five hundred words of profound." I can't quote Doug, since he owns copyright on his own material, but I can paraphrase. One night we went to fish the Hex hatch on the Betsie, but the river was high and dirty and we bailed out about eleven o'clock, when it was apparent that the hatch was not going to come off, and drove as fast as we could to the Platte. We hit the bridge just as a couple of guys were coming out of the water. Good hatch, big fish, they said, but we were too late. Yet even as they talked, Doug and I could hear fish feeding downstream. It was a blue-moon night—the second full moon of June—and so bright we never had to turn on our flashlights. We walked down through somebody's yard, then started wading slowly upstream, casting to fish feeding on stray spinners. We fished beside an old boathouse, by lawns mowed to the river's edge, with current lines waving lazily under the moon. I imagined it was like poaching on England's River Test, although I've never seen the River Test. Doug missed a big fish, and I took a sixteen-incher in slack water behind a shrub. The trout had risen so quietly that it made just a dimple on the surface. I cast above it and in the moonlight could see my fly the entire drift. It went under silently, as if pulled down by the hackles.

Later, when the spinner fall finally ended, Doug and I stood on the bridge and watched a movie playing silently on the screen of the drive-in across the field. At intermission the screen displayed the same crudely animated advertisements Doug and I watched when we were in high school twenty-five years ago. Doug was silent awhile and then said he found it amazing that an inaudible movie screen could conjure up such powerful associations. He said it took him back to dates with girls he had nearly forgotten. He swore he could smell Heaven Scent perfume and buttered popcorn. Life is very strange, he said, but the mysteries of the universe are nothing compared to being at a drive-in late in the second feature, in your father's car, with a fragrant girlfriend who allows you to unhook her bra for the first time.

A good fishing buddy cultivates a sense of wonder.

One of my newest fishing buddies is Pat Moore, who moved to Michigan from Colorado, where he'd worked for ten years as a fly-fishing guide, and went to work guiding out of Kelly's shop. Pat won me over right away with his good nature and by saying things like "Some guy comes rolling up in a Cadillac as big as *Guam,* I mean this guy had more money than *God,* and hired me for a day on the Au Sable. He caught six baby trout, not one of them over eight inches, and at the end of the day he said it was the most fun he'd had in thirty years."

One evening we were floating the Boardman, and Pat pointed to a spot where a few days earlier a client had hooked a giant brown trout. The client was a first-timer still learning how to cast. He had hurled a big streamer approximately where Pat told him to hurl it, and when the current swept it toward a leaning willow, the trout charged from beneath the branches and smashed the fly. The client set the hook but immediately lost control of his reel. While he fumbled for the handle, the fish ran off with a hundred yards of line and backing, accelerated in fast water below the next bend, and got off. Brown trout are not known for making such long runs. Keep pressure on them and they usually fight where they stand. Pat thought it would have gone twenty-six or twenty-seven inches.

I've fished that portion of the river hundreds of times without seeing a trout even nearly that big. Every time I've fished there I've made at least one cast with streamers, dry flies, wet flies, or nymphs to that dark hollow beneath the willow, and I have never caught a fish. I've caught a few nice ones just below that spot and a couple from the elbow bend above, but I've never caught a twenty-incher in that stretch, let alone a trout big enough to empty a free-spooling reel.

Pat had no history with the river, and maybe that was the

key. To him every overhanging branch and every jumble of submerged log was a place that could (and very likely does) hide a trout. Now he's convinced that huge browns live in every pool in the river. "I love the Boardman," he said, blasting a streamer to the bank with so much gusto that the boat rocked. "I'm all over this river like a rash. I wish I'd been fishing it all my life."

A good fishing buddy is enthusiastic.

I could go on, about buddies old and new, from my father, who has taken me fishing for forty years and still has much to teach; to Mike McCumby, one of the finest companions I've ever known on a stream; to Jerry Wilson, an accomplished chef who earned his living for years as a bouncer in a bar and as a professional arm wrestler, and is both a very good fisherman and a very good guy to have on your side; to Tom Hall and the gang at the Ginger Quill, who live and fish with dignity, grace, and good humor and are tolerant even of barbarians who stick butcher knives in the kitchen wall; to Craig Date, who when he was a beginner hauled in a five-pound smallmouth bass hand over hand because he had reeled his reel the wrong way and produced a horrible backlash, then tossed the bass on shore, stood over it, and asked, "Is it a big one?"

Good fishing friends are hard to come by, but they tend to last. You build a history together, and the friendship gets richer and deeper with every season. Last October, Kelly and I walked into the Platte and fished the Doctor's Hole for steelhead. The hole is named for the old M.D., now dead, who built a fishing shack under the pines there. He and his friends fished the Platte for decades, in the days when that small, clear river was one of the best trout streams in the state, long before it was overrun by Pacific salmon and overused by fishermen. When one of his buddies died, the doctor and another friend erected a stone monument that stands beside the river to this day. It reads:

IN MEMORY OF
RALPH R. KIMBALL
1878 1950
ARDENT FISHERMAN
AND CHERISHED
COMPANION BY HIS FRIENDS,
CHARLES L. PATTON M.D.
CHRISTOPHER PARNALL M.D.
1951

Kelly and I fished the pool until dark, then decided to go home. On our way out we saw a light shining in the shack and on impulse walked up on the porch and knocked. A man about our age came to the door, and we introduced ourselves. He shook our hands and said he was Jeff Parnall, a grandson of the man who had built the cabin. He was here on one of his regular visits from his home in upstate New York. Like us he had found no steelhead in the river. When Kelly reminded him that they had met a few years earlier, under circumstances much like these, he invited us inside for a drink.

We warmed up by the woodstove and looked around. It was a lovely fishing cabin, just big enough to sleep four on stacked bunks, with fly rods hanging on nails, rusted steelhead flies stuck in the windowsills, shelves crammed with books, souvenir ashtrays, whiskey bottles, and candles. The walls were decorated with art prints clipped from calendars and with framed black-and-white photos of the old doctor and his friends. The men in the photos belonged to a generation that wore neckties when they went fishing. They stood stiffly, staring without smiling into the camera, wearing tweed jackets and gentleman hats and holding bamboo rods. In the background was the shack with its board siding clean and new, and the river glinting silver through the pines. If you looked closely at their faces, you could see light in their eyes, could detect restrained mirth behind the rigid poses. Kelly noticed too. We exchanged looks. These were the guys who came before us, who fished here before we were even born, and of course the times were very different then but the people were not.

Jeff opened a cupboard and took down his grandfather's old shot glasses and a bottle of his favorite brand of bourbon, and we drank toasts to the people who came before us. We drank toasts to ourselves also, and to the Platte, and to the steelhead that ran up it and the brown trout that lived in it. We drank more toasts than were necessary, but none of us wanted the evening to end. Jeff put more wood in the stove, and we took turns telling stories about great days of fishing and the friends we had shared them with. We told stories until the whiskey was gone, then we went outside and stood by the river and told some more.

The Music Out There

ASIDE FROM CRAIG DATE, WHO WHILE HE'S CANOEING likes to sing a rousing rendition of "Love Is a Many-Splendored Thing," most of my friends prefer being quiet when they're outdoors. It's a virtue I embrace, in theory at least. I've learned that when I refrain from talking, banging gunwales, snapping branches, and howling at the sky, I become more aware of my surroundings, see more wildlife, and am more likely to still the senseless inner chatter that fills my head most of the time.

Usually when we say we want peace and quiet we don't mean peace and silence. We want the absence of noise, not the absence of sound. Seeking relief from television blare and traffic roar, we turn to quiet music, the rustle of wind in trees, birdsong, and, most soothing of all, water. Nothing puts us at ease so quickly as rain on a roof, the rumble of ocean surf, and the whispering of a river. When we surround ourselves with such sounds, it doesn't take long to start hearing the music out there.

I forgot that lesson one night while fishing the Hex hatch on the Boardman with Glenn and Doug. There was a decent spinner fall that night, but the river was crowded and the crowd was noisy. It was a full moon, so maybe there was something in the air. Hoots and yodels wafted down from a party on a sandbar a few bends upstream. The moon was so bright that it threw our shadows across the bottom of the river and we could change flies without flashlights. We watched anglers walking down the path toward the river when they were still a hundred yards away.

I had never seen so many people on the river. Doug took position at one bend, Glenn at another, I at a third. I thought we had the stretch sewn up, but three guys came late and squeezed between us. At first it didn't matter. Fish rose freely in every pool and behind every log and leaning cedar. I hooked a nice trout first cast in a small eddy tight to the bank, but it got off before I could tell if it was fourteen inches or twenty. Later I moved downstream and watched Doug cast to a fish that fed with obsessive, noisy regularity in the deepest pool in that part of the river. As Doug fished, one of the latecomers eased closer and closer, making short feigned casts to empty water. Finally he stood fifteen feet from Doug's elbow and stayed there, apparently hoping he could move in on Doug's trout.

I was giddy from a hard day's work and a little short-tempered. Being under a full moon, with a party warbling in the night, and surrounded by so many fishermen stumbling around on water I irrationally considered my own put me in a strange mood. I became unusually talkative. I talked directly to the encroacher beside Doug, lecturing him about river etiquette. I told him what I had been told many years earlier: If you're close enough to be heard in a normal tone of voice, you're too close. I told him that even during the Hex hatch, when trout are supposed to be lulled into confidence by the darkness and the abundance of insects, they can be put down for the night by a clumsy cast or by an inconsiderate interloper getting too damned close. I talked about other nights during the hatch, other fish on this stretch of the river, about the days before our time when Traverse City anglers would take the train to the old Beitner Dam—it washed out in a storm in 1961, but its wreckage is still visible beside the rapids—and camp for two or three days to fish this section of river that we can now drive to in five minutes. I told him Gordy Charles's story about the night watchman at the dam who used to prop his rod in the window above the spillway and lower a gob of nightcrawlers into the river below and catch brown trout so big he had to haul them home in wheelbarrows. I told him about the time Bud Haywood fished under Beitner Bridge on opening morning and caught a limit of trout on Mepps spinners—the smallest eighteen inches long and the biggest twenty-four. I talked so much that finally the guy backed off. He turned and headed downstream. The last thing he said was, "Doesn't that son of a bitch ever shut his yap?"

Well, yes, occasionally. A few nights later, fishing the Hex hatch on another river, I was reminded how rewarding it can be to stay quiet. After the hatch had ended, while wading slowly down the middle of the river and concentrating on being as alert as possible, I heard a disturbance near the bank: a faint push of water, quiet as a heron's step. I waited until I heard it again, a nearly silent sip, then saw a scribble of reflected light on the surface. There was enough moon still to throw shadows and to make every wrinkle in the river catch light. I cast once and watched out of the corner of my eye as my fly drifted to the spot and disappeared. I raised my rod and hooked the biggest trout of the night. I landed it, released it, and continued at the same slow pace downstream. A hundred feet along I heard another riser just as quiet as the first, and I caught that one too. There were no parties on the river that night, but I could hear fireworks in Elk Rapids popping like champagne corks one hotel room over.

Being quiet is such a natural ancillary to being on the water that by the time we start sagging and graying, it's often become automatic. Kids don't get it, which is why fathers insist so loudly on silence and have so little patience with infractions. I consider it a minor victory every time I convince a child to get quiet enough to notice birdcalls and frog racket. It was a big moment when my son Nick, at age six, spoke up after a silence to announce that a mourning dove sounds exactly like somebody blowing gently over the top of a Coke bottle.

You have to open yourself to natural spectacle, but willing it to happen is as difficult as willing yourself to fall in love. Like a child, you have to be empty of expectation, have to possess eyes that see and ears that hear. It takes practice, like anything. Sometimes you can be surprised.

One afternoon during a leisurely canoe trip down the Boardman, I shut my eyes for relief from the sun and became aware of a complex background of sounds I had missed until then. Such moments sometimes make me crazed with alertness: I want to listen with every cell of my skin, see with my palms, taste with my nipples and toes. I don't want to miss *anything,* and so, of course, blinded by a kind of sensory frenzy, I miss almost everything.

But that afternoon I listened to the canoe slip through the water with a sound like silk being torn, accompanied by a great deal of quiet hissing, humming, and chuckling. The river itself was a symphony of slurs and murmurs, distant throbbing, and much hushed gurgling, gulping, and grumbling. I dipped my paddle into the water, and it started a separate melody line, a rhythmic sip and swallow, followed by the swishing draw of the blade being pulled and a rhythmic dripping when I lifted it.

I don't believe that every encounter with nature automatically transports us back to some mystical sense of well-being stolen away by modern life. No doubt people have been inattentive and distracted as long as we've had the brains to string thoughts together. But I know that we're equipped to see and hear more than we usually do and that sometimes, when conditions are right, we can open ourselves to a world so rich with sensations that it makes the booming progress of civilization dim to insignificance.

Drifting downstream that afternoon, I realized that there's a big difference between hearing and listening. Hearing is passive; listening is active. We hear traffic and airport noise and the shouting loudspeakers in a department store. We listen to laughing children and hooting doves, to leaves rustling in wind-stirred aspens, to trout sipping mayflies in a river. In these noisy times the thousand subtle voices of a river can throw a calm over our lives. I swear it's music to our ears.

Eight Days of Hendricksons

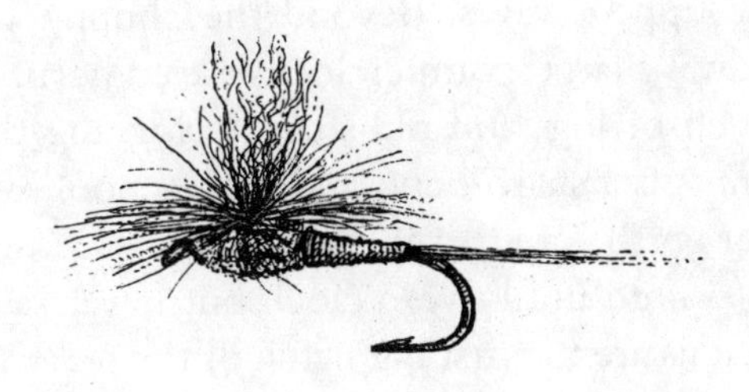

May 13

ON BLIND FAITH, BY CALENDAR RECKONING ALONE, I DROVE to the river and hiked a mile downstream from the bridge to the riffle I call Red Cabin. I had never fished here during the Hendrickson hatch, but the previous summer, while I floated this stretch with Kelly, he nodded at the water and said, "Good Hennie riff. Big fish." Kelly's cryptic comments are usually significant. When he nods at a pool or a logjam and says a big fish lives there, it's because he has direct knowledge of it, having recently seen or hooked or released it. Often all three. The riffle below the redwood-colored cabin stuck in my mind. I thought of it all winter.

The day was classic May in Michigan: cold in the morning,

warming to the low sixties by noon, the wind blowing scraps of clouds across the sun. The woods were gray and brown, the buds on the trees closed tight as fists. It would take a warm rain and two days of sunshine to make leaves appear.

The water was higher than I wanted, and dark. To get to the riffle I crossed the river twice at flats that in summer are hip deep. Now the water topped my waders and ran in an icy burn down my waist.

I waded cautiously to the edge of the riffle. The current was stronger than I expected; my boots threatened to roll across gravel like cargo on skids. My side of the river was smooth, but the slick surface was misleading. I knew I could never cross it. At midstream the surface was choppy with white-tipped waves. Beyond the choppy water, a long cast away, was a large, counterclockwise eddy, running tight against a bunch of logs and old stumps clogging the far shore. Upstream was a sharp bend and a deep pool, with the red cabin sitting on the crest of the bank above it.

I waited until five o'clock but never saw a mayfly. Hendricksons are the first big hatch of the season, and notoriously unreliable. Walking back to the bridge, I met an angler on the trail. He seemed lost, stopping now and then to peer under the cedars at the river. When I asked if he had seen any Hendricksons, he said, "Hendricksons?"

May 14

DOUG AND I fished the riffle at Red Cabin, but it was a bright day, and Hendricksons rarely emerge when the sun is out. By three o'clock we had seen only a few duns scooting past on the wind, and no rising trout. Doug finally tied on a black Woolly Bugger and waded to the edge of the pool at the bend above the riffle. The water there is deep, perhaps eight feet, and drops off from a sand ledge on the upstream side. It's a place for big trout.

But Doug made a mistake. He cut off his dry fly and tied the streamer directly to the end of his tapered leader, where the tippet was about three-pound test. He should have cut the leader back three or four feet, to six-pound test at least. But he was being lazy. Or he was thinking that should the Hendricksons start hatching after all, he would be ready to switch quickly to dries again. Or he could not bring himself to chop a four-dollar leader in half. Or he had no faith in the fly or the water and figured it wouldn't matter.

He cast the streamer into the pool. He stripped once and something large came up, engulfed the fly, and broke the tippet. The swirl it made was so large it drifted downstream for thirty feet before dissipating. Doug looked at me. "Damn," he said. "Damn, damn, damn."

May 15

I SUGGESTED THAT Glenn stand at the top of the pool and keep an eye on the place where Doug had cast his doomed streamer. He stripped twenty feet of line from his reel and started casting a parachute Hendrickson for practice. I waded a hundred feet downstream, to the middle of the riffle, and glanced back at Glenn. A nice trout bounced end over end in front of him.

When I got there the trout was on its side on the surface. It was an eighteen-inch brown with deep, rich colors and bold spots. Glenn tried to lead it a little closer to shore, where I could reach it, and at that moment it rolled over, and the fly shot from its mouth. The trout righted itself and swam with a bit of a wobble into deep water.

Glenn described what happened. At the end of one of his practice casts, he had let his fly drag in the water until it went under. It was swimming in a straight line below him when the trout came up and took it.

Later a few Hendrickson duns appeared on the surface, rode for a few moments with their dark wings held high like sails, then flew off. A trout flicked the surface of the riffle, but only once.

May 16

IN THE NIGHT it rained. The river comes up fast during a rain, and the fishing can be extraordinary if you happen to be there while the water is rising. It's a good time to throw streamers against the banks. You want them to streak through the darkening water, and you'd better use a stout leader.

But I was too late. I reached the river at noon, and it was already as high as it would get and too dark to fish. When I stood on the bridge looking at the water below, a gust blew my hat off and it floated downstream. Two guys fishing bait at the bend saw it and tried to snag it as it went past, but they missed. I waved to them and they waved back.

May 17

AT NOON I met Kelly, and we hiked to a section of the upper river neither of us had fished in years. This far upstream the river had not been blown out by the rain. It was clear and wadable, glinting gray beneath an overcast sky. It wound in lazy curves across a mile-long band of meadow—a rare stretch of open river in this country of woods and swamps. Hendricksons flew past with the wind. Others sailed on the water. As we rigged up, the wind gusted harder, and pellets of rain drove at an angle to the ground.

The hatch got heavier. Mayflies drifted on the current seams, one every few feet, and rising trout showed everywhere up and down the river. When a hatch is on, it always seems inevitable and continuous, the usual state of affairs. It's easy to imagine that you can come back to the river anytime and find trout rising confidently in every run and pool. If you never saw it again, you would remember this little river winding through the meadow as a place where trout rose every day to Hendricksons.

We walked the banks and took turns casting to feeding trout. The rain turned to sleet, then to wet flakes of snow that clumped together as they fell and struck the water with audible splashes. Trout fed until the hatch ended late in the afternoon, when the woods and fields were covered with a soggy coat of white. We discovered during the walk back to the truck that we were wet and cold.

In the tavern in Fredric, we ordered coffee and beer and watched hockey highlights on the television over the bar. The Red Wings were in the finals, on their way to their first Stanley Cup in forty-two years. We ordered giant burritos and more beer and flirted with the waitress, who was not impressed. She was a lifer. Nothing we could have said or done would have surprised her.

"You guys been swimming, or what?" she asked.

"Fishing," we said.

While we waited for our meal, Kelly told me about the May a few years ago when he guided on the river eighteen days in succession without seeing a Hendrickson hatch. The hatch should have been on, but every day was sunny, and the bugs refused to emerge. Then, the nineteenth day, low clouds covered the sky, and in the afternoon duns started popping and suddenly trout were rising everywhere. The clients were beginners who had never experienced such a hatch. They could do nothing wrong. Trout twelve to eighteen inches long gobbled every fly they threw at them. The clients caught so many that they lost count. They also lost all of Kelly's flies. They were finally reduced to using flies brought along by one of the clients—mass-produced Japanese cheapos with oversize quill wings and webby hackle the color of an old lady's bad hairdo, the kind of flies you find for sale in plastic bubble packs in the fishing department at K Mart. But it didn't matter to the trout. They couldn't get enough of those imitations of imitations.

The waitress came with our burritos. They were big enough to use as clubs.

"Fishing," she said. "Funny. You guys don't look that stupid."

May 18

ALONE, ALL MY friends working, I return to Red Cabin and stand at the edge of the riffle. I watch the water so intently that the trees on shore swoon upstream around me. There is something like an electrical charge in the air, a sense of imminence. The wind is down, the sky gray with patches of blue, and the air temperature is sixty-five degrees, the warmest day of the spring so far. Something's about to happen.

I wade into the fast water, until gravel moves under my feet, making crunching sounds like ice cubes being chewed. I like the slight edge of danger. I like perching on a moment knowing it is about to end. Something is going to happen, and you never know what. The mayflies are scarce, but at any moment they might break free in an outburst of plenitude. My fly, if cast well, could be mistaken for an insect and taken in a greedy slurp by a trout so large and wary that no human has seen it in the four or five years it has terrorized baitfish and picked off bugs in this riffle.

The sun goes behind a cloud, and duns appear. First they are in the air, flying downstream, looking enormous against the gray sky—clumsy and graceful at once, like lumberjacks doing ballet. Then they are on the water, riding the current with their wings up. And trout begin to feed.

This goes on all afternoon. Each time a cloud blots the sun and the light goes gray, mayflies appear instantly, whole flotillas of them bobbing downstream on the riffle, and trout begin slashing and rolling where a moment ago there were no living things. The trout feed viciously, as if knowing that the bounty won't last. They come up fast, going down and coming up again five seconds later, grabbing as many mayflies as they can. In the eddy the trout follow a tight circuit, around and around, stitching the surface with their riseforms. If my cast is off by a few inches, the fly drifts past the rising trout and is caught in the fast water and pulled away. But if the cast is right—if the line unfurls and the fly lands behind loose curves of leader in the current seam—the drift is drag free, and there is a good chance a trout will take. The trout are lined up where the water makes a wall between the fast current and the slow, where they can stay in position without much effort and watch the procession of insects coming down from above. They take my artificials with exactly the same confidence they take the naturals, a bold lightning grab like a dog snapping a housefly in flight. My fly is a parachute Hendrickson on a size 14 hook, with a bronze wing and split tail. It is the same pattern that worked yesterday on the upper river.

I hook and land three brown trout: a seventeen-incher, then a sixteen-incher, then an eighteen-incher. Another rolls over the top of my fly, and when I raise my rod to set the hook it goes deep into the fold of flesh where the pectoral fin meets the body. The trout flares sideways to the current and bucks like a kite. I assume it is twenty inches, maybe twenty-two, but it is barely sixteen. By the time I work the fly out of its fin and release it, the hatch is over.

May 19

At certain moments of certain days, sometimes predictable, sometimes not, a kind of switch is flipped, and thousands of insects crawl from gravel or silt on the bottom of the river and swim frantically to the surface, where they undergo a metamorphosis into graceful winged creatures that ride the surface for a moment, then launch into flight. The event trips another switch: Trout follow the insects to the surface and feast.

Today begins like a feast day. Low slate-colored clouds

cover the sky and trap humid air against the earth. There is expectancy everywhere. It's one of those days when you think: Sure thing. If the Hendricksons hatched yesterday, they'll hatch today. You're sure of it. Big hatch, big fish. It's a day for hogs.

When you fish the same spot in a river day after day, you get to know the bottom intimately. Two steps out from the end of the sunken log (half buried like a speed bump; you nearly fell the first time you kicked it), past a patch of sand, to the eddy behind the rock, then veer hard against the current upstream and across for five or six difficult steps until you're at the place where the bottom drops away. The river piles against your belly. You feel the loss of gravity until you reach a balance between your submerged half and your exposed half. To stay there you must lock the muscles in your thighs and calves and lean into the river. After twenty minutes your legs begin to tremble.

Casting is awkward. You twist your torso downstream and lift the trailing line into the air. You make one short backcast that straightens the line, unfurling it behind you in the space between tag alders on the bank, then a snappy forward cast that propels the line forty feet across the current, with a last-second upstream reach so the fly will touch down below the leader and drift for three or four feet before the line straightens and drags the fly. It sounds more complicated than it is. Once you've learned, it's mostly automatic, like fingers finding chords on a guitar.

Late in the afternoon a few Hendrickson spinners do their puppet dance over the riffle, but no trout feed. You wade to shore and walk into the woods looking for morels. You find none, so you go home.

May 20

I'M WAIST DEEP at the edge of the riffle, thinking that a rising fish stirs the predator in us. An angler casting to a feeding trout moves like a feline. He stalks one step at a time, never taking his eyes off the spot where the fish showed, then casts and holds his breath while the fly rides the current into the feeding lane and is accepted or rejected.

Such moments of concentration can be a kind of meditation or prayer, a doorway to the antechamber, at least, of the sublime. When your concentration is complete, layers of residue are stripped away. Ordinary concerns get lathered off, and the alluvium of daily living is swept downstream. Spend two hours intent on a single purpose, and the world leans toward you and says, "Look at me." You look, and what you see sustains you through a week of telephone calls, traffic snarls, and meetings run by unctuous devotees of Robert's Rules of Order.

Outside it's easy to abandon every convention and prejudice and get down to the messy business of being an animal, alive. When you're rooting around in the water or the woods, miles from the nearest strip mall and office complex, nobody is likely to judge you by your clothing or your skin color or your political orientation, and if they do you don't give a damn anyway. Fishing—or hunting or photographing birds or cutting firewood—frees you of such nonsense. If you want society, convention, comfort, and safety, stay home. If you want your life to be a joyous romp, get outside.

Then I see mayflies in the air. They are flying with gathering purpose in a flight a few inches to a dozen feet above the water. And trout are rising to them. Their sipping rises become slashing rises, and two large fish begin feeding with outrageous gulping eruptions that seem to devour chunks of the river itself.

It's a gray day, a Hendrickson day, and I'm alone at Red Cabin, at the right place at the right time with the right fly and all afternoon ahead of me. A third big trout begins to feed. I take two steps deeper into the river, to the verge of disaster, and strip line. I wish my friends were here to share this. I cast, and the Hendrickson imitation touches down five feet above a riser. The fly looks good on the water, the dark wings upright, the size and color right, the drift natural.

The sun tries to break free, but clouds move in to cover it. When they do, the sky closes, the river opens, and my fly disappears.

Something Big

YOU CAN ONLY STAY GOOD FOR SO LONG. THAT SPRING I was exemplary: a faithful husband, a model father, a dry-fly purist so devoted to the ethics and aesthetics of the sport that I deserved to be sainted, bronzed, and mounted on a pedestal next to Theodore Gordon. For weeks I'd been fishing mayfly hatches in the skinny rivers near home. I fished only during gentleman's hours, then again briefly in the evening during the spinner fall—and released every fish I caught. Every damned one.

But the pressure to be good was too great, and I started having impure thoughts. The world had become too tame for me. It lacked mystery and flavor and the spice of illicit pleasures. I imagined twelve-inch brookies sputtering in butter in a skillet. I daydreamed about walking into the Troutsman dragging a brown trout I'd cracked on the skull with a baseball bat. I started longing for a knock-down-drag-out brawl with a muskie or northern pike. To hell with gentility, I decided. I wanted bleeding knuckles and flying snot.

So when Tom Carney phoned one evening in June and started babbling about night fishing for pig-size walleyes, I listened. Tom's a writer and a high school English teacher, the kind who goes to work early every morning and grades papers at home every evening and lies awake at night worrying about the slackers who slouch in the back row of his classroom. When the school year ends, Tom is always in serious need of a vacation. Now his mood matched mine exactly. He wanted to catch unsophisticated fish with unsophisticated methods. He wanted to fill an ice chest with fillets and fry them in beer batter. He wanted to fish at night, on water deep enough to hide mysteries, where he might hook something so big he had no chance of landing it. I asked if he had any place in particular in mind, and he said North Dakota. I started packing.

We drove the interstates west and didn't stop until we bumped up against the Missouri River near Bismarck. Prairie stretched taut from horizon to horizon, and the river flowed strong and calm, the color of molten clay. Upstream, Lake Sakakawea sprawled across the state like a vast taproot.

In Mandan, Tom and I asked around for someone who could show us a thing or two about catching walleye at night and were introduced to a softspoken young man named Keith Christianson, a railroad engineer by profession and a fishing guide weekends, evenings, and holidays. He had been fishing the Missouri and its impoundments most of his life.

"Sure, we can fish after dark," he said, but he hesitated as he said it. I've heard that same hesitation in the voices of guides on Saginaw Bay, Lake Erie, and other places where walleyes grow big and abundant. It was a way of saying, "Yeah, we can fish at night, but the fishing's so good during the day, why bother?"

That evening we launched Keith's aluminum boat into the Missouri below Garrison Dam and drifted downstream between striated clay banks that turned to flaming ocher as the sun set. We fished the snag-infested bottom with whole nightcrawlers on Lindy Rigs—a wire dropper-and-sinker arrangement popular in the Midwest—and caught a half dozen walleye up to three pounds, a few sauger (the walleye's smaller cousin), and two small channel catfish. Tom and I were certain we would start hooking larger fish once night fell.

But as dusk sneaked up the valley, Keith started losing confidence. He was nervous about maneuvering his boat in the dark around the many snags and sandbars and decided we should motor upstream near the dam, where the water was deeper. He said large walleye were sometimes caught there at night, in the deep, turbulent pools below the turbines.

It was dark by the time we got there. We switched to Rapalas and fished the edge of the current in the half mile of river below the dam, trolling so close to the bank it was possible to reach out and tap dry gravel with the tips of our rods. We had occasional strikes and hooked a few walleye twelve to fifteen inches long, smaller even than the ones we had taken downstream on nightcrawlers. Once a lone fisherman standing on the bank cast across our stern, so close that his lure whistled past Keith's head. We had intruded on his territory. Keith made no comment, just steered us farther from shore.

The night was lit only by the Milky Way straight overhead; in the humid air the stars glittered like radiant gravel flung across black ice. We motored around a bend and there stood the dam: three immense, looming columns of white concrete illuminated by floodlights. They couldn't have seemed more out of place if they had been a trio of skyscrapers airlifted from

Chicago and dropped on the prairie. Swarms of insects spiraled around the lights. Bats and nighthawks swooped in and out of the beams like marauding fighter planes.

Below the dam the river was strong, the surface swelling with turbulence. I thought of the poet John Neihardt, who in 1908 floated most of the length of the Missouri River in a small boat and afterward wrote: "I love all things that yearn toward distant seas." A river as long as the Missouri has a powerful yearning. Riding the heaving current beneath the dam, I smelled mountain headwaters, sweet prairie grass, and salty ocean. It was a heady and primitive smell, one that cut across continents and centuries, and I wanted to follow it all the way down to the Mississippi and the Gulf of Mexico.

Suddenly there was a beating of wings, like sails luffing in a wind, and three large white pelicans flapped slowly out of the darkness thirty feet above our heads and glided toward the dam. In the lights they glowed a ghostly white that made them seem both prehistoric and timeless, like pterodactyls attracted across the ages. The scene had the searing quality of a light burned into your retina by a flashbulb. I glanced at Tom and Keith and they looked the way I felt: wide-eyed and speechless.

We stayed on the river until after midnight but caught nothing more. Enough night fishing, we decided. We would fish in daylight, in the reservoir, where Keith said there were walleye that could put a real bend in a rod.

EARLY THE NEXT morning we met for breakfast at a restaurant in Garrison. It was the kind of small-town café you expect to see patronized by farmers and retired cowboys, but it was filled instead with tanned men in jeans and gimme hats talking about walleye fishing. On every wall were walleye mounted on enameled plaques. Most had weighed eight pounds or more. All had been caught in recent years from Lake Sakakawea.

Keith asked if we were willing to do some driving to get near the distant center of the lake, where he had heard from other guides that a lot of fish were being caught. We consolidated gear into Keith's truck and drove 40 miles to a public ramp, launched the boat, and motored up the lake into wind and rolling waves. The shores were barren of trees and sloped at flat angles into the water or ended at great eroding cliffs of stratified rock and clay. The land was colored entirely in grays and browns, the sky so blue it could have been cut into pieces and sold to tourists. We motored on, the spray from the waves blowing over the bow into our faces.

Lake Sakakawea is named for the Shoshone woman who was both guide and interpreter for Lewis and Clark during their expedition up the Missouri and across the Continental Divide to Oregon in 1804–6. The reservoir stretches 180 miles from the Montana border, where the Missouri and Yellowstone Rivers come together, to Garrison Dam, north of Bismarck. It is such a large body of water that fishermen tend to focus on one portion exclusively. They might fish for years among the islands and complex bays in the wide lower end, yet know nothing about the lake 50 miles closer to Montana. That strange water to the west might as well be another lake altogether.

Most anglers on Lake Sac are after walleye, sauger, and saugeye—a naturally occurring hybrid of the two—although the lake also supports smallmouth bass, white bass, northern pike, channel catfish, paddlefish, and king salmon. We caught a few small channel cats and a northern pike, but mostly we caught walleye. We caught them by trolling, casting, and drifting, in shallow water and over deep gravel bars, with jigs and crankbaits, with nightcrawlers, leeches, and minnows. Though we failed to hook any of the ten-pound and larger fish the lake is famous for, we caught many two- to four-pounders—so many we often fought two and sometimes three at the same time—and every one that measured over about eighteen inches went into the live well.

The steadiest action came after Keith steered us to a sunken reef in the middle of the reservoir, where a half dozen other boats were drift fishing jigs tipped with nightcrawlers and minnows. The procedure was to cut the motor at the windward side of the reef, where someone had planted a temporary marker buoy, throw out a sea anchor to slow the boat, then drift with the wind down the length of the reef, watching the depth locator as it marked sixty, forty, twenty, and finally twelve feet of water. The fish were at twelve feet. We handled two rods each, or tried to. Sometimes strikes came so quickly we could not put our second lines in the water.

Once as we motored upwind to begin another pass over the reef we noticed a man and a woman in a bass boat off by themselves in deep water. The man, sitting in the bow seat, held a deeply arched rod. A half hour later, when we circled around again, the boat was farther away and the man in the bow still held the bent rod. It occurred to us that he had been fighting the same fish the entire time. Keith pulled out a pair of binoculars and watched for a few minutes. "He's got a real hog on," he said.

Our next trip upwind we saw the woman in the stern standing with a landing net in her hands. Even from our distance we could see that the net was too small. We reeled in our lines and started toward them to see if we could help.

The man was in his late thirties or early forties, and not in the best of shape. It was midday by then, with the sun high and hot, but even in the heat and after more than an hour of exertion he appeared to be holding up well. He kept the rod high, the pressure steady on the fish, and seemed to know better than to get impatient and try to horse it. He used his feet to control an electric trolling motor that kept the boat moving slowly in the direction of the fish.

"Whatcha got?" Keith called as we came up slowly from the stern.

The man turned and appraised us. "I don't know. Something big."

"Want a bigger net?"

"You bet. Thanks. I don't know what I'm hooked to, but it's surely too big for our little net."

"What'd you hook it on?"

"A small spinner and minnow. When it hit it felt like it was going thirty miles an hour and planned to run straight on through to St. Louis. I think maybe it's a big pike. Or a paddlefish. I've only got six-pound-test line, but it's fresh, and I'm in no hurry. There's no place, in fact, I'd rather be right now."

We passed Keith's wide salmon net to the woman, then backed off slowly, and when we were far enough away to be clear in case the fish turned and ran our way, we shut off our motor and watched. The electronics showed we were in eighty feet of water. From the contours drawn on the graph it appeared that there was a sunken forest beneath us. Bizarre shapes rose ten and twenty feet from the bottom.

"A lot of snags down there," Keith called. "Don't let it go to the bottom."

The man glanced at us and shrugged. "I don't have much say in the matter."

Sometimes he gained line, pumping and reeling as his boat moved up on the fish. But then it would run, taking line in a high-pitched racheting whine. Holding his rod out, the tip bent nearly to the water, the man would allow the line to go until it seemed certain he would soon be down to bare spool. But the fish would eventually slow, and the man would pump the rod and get a little line back. He turned once, said something to the woman, and she held a can of soda to his mouth and he took a long drink.

We watched until it began to seem hopeless. I wondered if in his place I would have done the same, would have fought the fish long after there was much chance of landing it—of even seeing it—would have hung on out of stubbornness and pride and vestigial hope, like the old man in *The Old Man and the Sea*. There were mild heroics at work that day on Lake Sac, and I sensed we were witnessing something that lies close to the heart of angling, but frankly it got a little boring to watch. We went back to the reef. By then the man and woman were far from the other fishermen, their boat low and small in the distance. We kept track of them with the binoculars.

Finally, more than two hours after we first noticed them, they motored across the lake toward us. They came up beside our boat, smiling grimly and shaking their heads. The woman passed the big net back to Keith.

"It got down into something on the bottom," she said. "After all that time. And we never even saw it. We have no idea what it was."

"Maybe it was a big channel cat," Keith suggested.

"All I know," the man said, "is it was the biggest fish I ever hooked in fresh water and it beat me. We're heading home to Colorado now, but I'll tell you what: We'll be back."

Later, when the action slowed on the reef, we moved closer to shore and began casting lures along the drop-off. A very pissed-off northern pike of about six pounds slammed my crankbait and came out of the water throwing its head back and forth like a horse trying to get free of a rope. We had a brief but spirited exchange before Keith netted the pike and got it in the boat. I enjoy eating pike now and then, but we had already kept enough walleye to feed a battalion so we unhooked the northern with needlenose pliers and slid it back into the lake. It was our last fish of the day.

Tom and I had found the restorative we were looking for. We'd found a few bonuses besides. The ghost-white pelicans above the river and the Colorado angler's losing battle became images of almost mythological significance to us. They made the world seem new again, rich with potential and shot through with mystery. For weeks every river, creek, and pond would be vibrant with possibilities, and every cast would seem like the one that could hook something enormous and unstoppable.

That night we ate walleye fillets crispy with batter and drank a coolerful of cold beer. There wasn't a fresh vegetable in sight. By morning I was eager to go home and fish the brown drake hatch on the Manistee. It's not a big river, but it has pools plenty big enough to hide monsters.

Giants

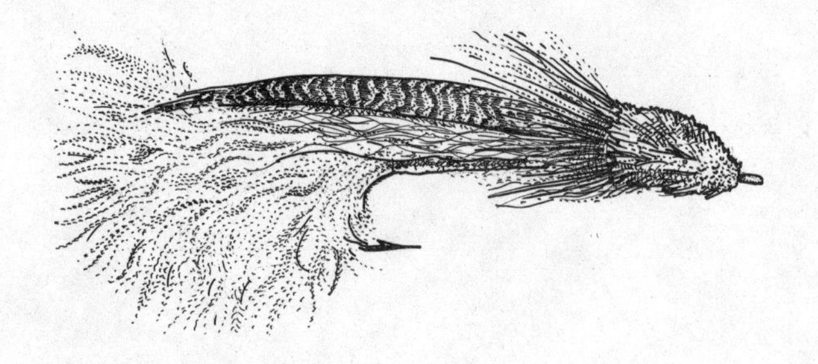

EVERY GAME FISH HAS A DIMENSION BEYOND WHICH IT becomes an exemplar, a paragon, a bragging fish. The dimensions vary, of course, according to species and place. Down South largemouth bass grow to the size of state-fair hogs, so it takes double-digit weight to be worthy of boasting. Here in the North, cold water and short summers make our bass reach trophy status at about six pounds. For smallmouths the defining number is five pounds; for northern pike, ten; for steelhead, fifteen. Chinook salmon don't raise eyebrows until they reach twenty-five or thirty pounds.

You have to keep some perspective on this. A one-pound bluegill deserves more praise than a four-pound walleye. And while a three-pound rainbow trout is a stud in the Au Sable, trollers on Lake Michigan dismiss it as small, a mere "skipper." Trout and salmon grow so big in the Great Lakes that they skew the grading curve. A three-pounder makes almost no impression when it's caught in company with twenty-pounders, especially when landed with tackle stout enough to drag a cow behind a train. But a wild three-pound trout in a river is another matter.

On most rivers where I've fished, a sixteen-inch trout is considered a nice fish, an eighteen-incher is a *nice* fish, and anything bigger is worthy of hosannas. For years a twenty-incher was such an elusive prize that I remember at age twenty being disappointed when I caught a brown trout that measured nineteen and three-quarter inches. Since then I've taken a fair number of browns, rainbows, and even brook trout bigger than twenty inches, but most of them were caught in places like southern Chile, which hardly counts, or were taken at night during the *Hexagenia* hatch, when big trout are more vulnerable than usual. A twenty-inch resident trout from a Michigan river, on a fly, in daylight, when I could see the strike and watch the battle and admire the colors of the fish—that was an experience that eluded me until I had fished those rivers for twenty years. You might say I finally earned the right, though I'm sure it had more to do with chance. For a long time my luck was bad, then it got better. Throw a fly into the water enough times, and eventually even the biggest fish comes down with a case of the stupids.

After a trout reaches about twenty inches, it's more convenient to scale it in pounds, yet most anglers I know in Michigan measure even their largest trout by the inch. That might be because we don't want those trout associated with the ten- and twenty-pounders we see caught so frequently from the Great Lakes and displayed dead on the dock. Also, those of us who prefer to release most or all of our trout—even, and perhaps especially, the big ones—can rarely take the time to weigh fish. We measure them quickly and get them back into the water. When a lady in Grayling recently caught a very large brown trout during the Hex hatch, it was the length of the fish—thirty inches—that everyone talked about, not the weight. Saying it was a ten-pounder would have lacked punch.

Thirty-inchers are extremely hard to come by, but you can't believe how many twenty-inchers are caught. Literally: You can't believe it. I've seen so many seventeen-inchers grow to twenty that I've become skeptical of every report. Kelly Galloup, who in his shop hears stories almost daily about twenty-inch trout taken from area waters, automatically subtracts two or three inches. He's been fishing the rivers around here all his life and has caught more big trout than anyone I know. He understands just how big a genuine twenty-incher is, and how rare.

Not that they don't exist. They do, and probably in greater numbers than most people suspect. The twenty-inch benchmark has taken on quasi-mythical status on many waters, which is why so many anglers chase small trout while harboring secret hope of the unexpected whopper. According to that way of thinking, a large trout is an anomaly, like an albino moose or a zucchini the size of a couch. A lot of people are convinced that such trout, even if they do exist, are so smart they're virtually uncatchable.

It's not unusual for anglers to admit at a certain period in their lives that they've given up the quest for big trout, that they care less about the size of the fish than the quality of the experience, that they appreciate a ten-inch brook trout more than a ten-pound brown trout. I can sympathize. I was once like that. My lust to kill faded and never came back, and I long ago lost any urge to demonstrate prowess. Yet I'm more interested in large trout now than at any time in my life. In my youth I caught some decent fish, but few giants. Now, after thirty years of apprenticeship, I'm arrogant enough to believe that I can occasionally catch one.

Mere bulk is not enough. I like catching steelhead, salmon, northern pike, muskie, bass, even carp when they can be caught in clean water on light tackle, and I will probably shout tributes at the top of my voice for tarpon, bonefish, and striped bass if I ever wet my feet in salt, but I would still rather catch wild, river-dwelling trout than any other fish. I'll take a twenty-inch brown trout any day over a twenty-pound king salmon. It's a matter of temperament. On the waters where I fish, salmon are aliens, transported across the continent from the Pacific Northwest, entering rivers not to feed but to complete brief and ultimately fatal mating missions. Catching them is like setting an ambush. Brown trout are aliens, too—as I am—but they have been here long enough to become nationalized—as I have also. They live year round in the rivers, and know their surroundings intimately. When you step into a river, you're stepping into their kitchen. Catching them requires knowledge of the kitchen, the seasons, the insects, crustaceans, and baitfish—requires knowing almost as much as the trout. You can sometimes get lucky, but to be consistently lucky you have to be good.

Kelly is one of the best you'll ever meet. It's not quite accurate to say he's a big-fish specialist—I've watched him spend many hours casting dry flies to eight-inch brookies—but much of his time on the water is spent targeting giants. His success at catching them is partly due to the fact that he sees through the many misconceptions and bits of untested conventional wisdom that bog down so many anglers. The first summer we fished together, I mentioned something about big brown trout feeding primarily at night. That nugget of information is gospel in every how-to book in my library and is a staple of fly-fishing seminars everywhere. I've heard it all my life. And since I had caught so few big brown trout during the day, it was easy to believe they didn't feed until midnight.

Kelly listened without comment. The next day he drove me to a stretch of the Manistee that is among the most heavily fished on that popular river. We waded downstream, at noon, on a bright Thursday in early July. Kelly rigged a six-weight rod and reel with a full-sinking line, a type-six Cortland 444 Rocket Taper. I don't ordinarily endorse products, but that particular line is so well suited to the way Kelly fishes that it deserves mention. It is much smaller in diameter than most sinking lines, which allows it to sink quickly, yet it is light enough and flexible enough to cast easily. Ease of casting is crucial when you're fishing streamers the way Kelly does. He casts with pinpoint accuracy to specific structure in the river, and does it for hours at a time. Lead-core lines are too heavy and clumsy for the job.

Right away Kelly destroyed another cherished myth about brown trout. While I tied a small bucktail streamer to a nine-foot leader tapering to four-pound tippet, he knotted a one-foot section of twenty-pound test to his line, added a one-foot midsection of ten-pound test, and finished with a foot-long tippet of eight-pound test to which he attached a very large, bulky streamer. His total leader was three feet long and strong enough to land tarpon. When I expressed surprise, Kelly said he's convinced that a trout charging a streamer is motivated as much by territorial imperative as by hunger, and that in either case the trout is not looking at the leader. With dry flies, yes, they can be extraordinarily leader shy, but if a trout is intent on killing an intruder, it will attack whether the intruder is attached to a leader testing two pounds or twelve. A heavy leader also makes it possible to land the fish quickly so it can be easily resuscitated and released.

We waded downstream, and Kelly cast his big streamer tight to the bank, slapping it as close as possible to sunken logs, stumps, overhanging bushes, and every other place that offered cover. He slapped the water with the fly because he's found that brown trout, like largemouth bass, are attracted to such stimuli. The moment the fly hit the water, he began stripping it back, causing it to swim rapidly downstream, a couple of feet beneath the surface, darting like a sculpin or other baitfish trying to get the hell out of Dodge.

I went first, fishing my conventional rig, and in an hour caught several twelve-inchers. Kelly followed immediately behind, close enough to chat, and cast into the same water I had covered, but tighter to the bank and just above or below the deep pools, especially in places where sunken debris and beds of weeds made microhabitats in two or three feet of quick current. Where I had caught nothing, he caught a twenty-inch brown and an eighteen-inch brown. I became a believer.

Kelly's tactics have changed my entire approach to trout fishing. I still prefer fishing to risers during a hatch, but I'm no longer disappointed when there are no risers. Most of the time, after all, there aren't. And since I'm not content to spend my time waiting for bugs to appear, I've become a maniac for streamers. I fish them all day long. My casting hand is nearly as callused as it was when I swung a hammer for a living. And I'm catching more big trout than ever. Not as many as Kelly—this student will probably never match his teacher in skill—but more than I ever expected to catch.

The most efficient way to hunt big trout is in a boat, especially one that allows a casting angler to stand. We often use Kelly's McKenzie River drift boat, two or three of us taking turns rowing and casting, covering ten miles of river in eight hours. When you fish with Kelly, you have to be prepared to spend all day on the river making cast after cast after cast, each with deliberation and concentration, placed just so, the streamer slapping the water as close as possible to every bank, stump, and rock. The streamer's escape route takes it streaking past a sunken log or parallel bands of sand, mossy bottom, and shadow, or past the woven, algae-encrusted sticks drowned near a beaver lodge—places where giant trout stake out territory and guard it. We sometimes cast all day without a single strike. Or we have six strikes and land three fish. One or two will be about sixteen inches long. Another will be over eighteen inches. Once every three or four days one of us catches a trout over twenty inches. My biggest is twenty-three inches. Every season Kelly gets a couple over twenty-five.

Kelly, who is an innovative fly tier (his Troutsman Hex and Troutsman Drake are the best imitations I've ever used for *Hexagenia,* brown drakes, and *Isonychia* spinners), invented a streamer he calls the Zoo Cougar specifically for casting with sinking lines on rivers filled with structure. The writer Bob Linsenman, who's had some big days with that streamer, came up with the name after he decided the fly had the cynical and overfed look of a cougar confined all its life behind bars. It can be grouped with Muddler Minnows and other streamers constructed with heads of spun deer hair, but otherwise it's revolutionary. It's tied with a yellow marabou tail, gold tinsel body, and a wing of calf-tail hair, overlaid with a mallard flank feather dyed lemon and seated flat over the body, not edgewise as is traditional with most streamers. The head is deer-body hair dyed dark yellow, spun and trimmed loosely with a razor blade. The finished fly has a substantial profile and markings suggestive of a sculpin. Most important, the flat position of the wing and the broad deer-hair head cause the fly to swim in an undulating hula dance. There are days when trout will eat no other fly.

Kelly also likes big bucktail streamers dyed the brightest possible chartreuse, and bushy combinations of marabou and rabbit fur tied to give them a broad silhouette and enticing action. He dislikes using streamers weighted with lead wire or bead eyes, believing that unweighted flies are more lifelike in the water. And he likes them big, on the reasonable assumption that oversize flies attract oversize fish. When his marabou streamers are dry, fresh from the box, they look like Angora kittens charged with static electricity. As soon as they hit the water and sink, they come alive. It's a wonder any fish can resist them. Any fish, that is, big enough not to be afraid of them.

Casting big flies for trout is not for everyone. It's hard work, and it contradicts many of our favorite myths about fly-fishing—that it's a gentle sport for contemplative sorts, that purity of intentions and good equipment and careful application of your skills will be rewarded whether you catch fish or not, that big fish are beside the point. With streamers the way Kelly ties and fishes them, big fish are most emphatically the point. If you're the kind of person who needs constant reward, you'll get more satisfaction from catching small fish on dry flies. But I've discovered that I have a deep longing for trout capable of yanking the rod from my hand. Funny how eight hours of fruitless casting can be forgotten the moment a big brown or rainbow charges out of nowhere, turns, engulfs your streamer, and tries to drag you into the river.

All this is just prelude to what happened one day last year on the lower Au Sable, what Bob Linsenman calls his "crick." Bob, Kelly, and I were floating a stretch that has the broad sweeping bends of a western river and is known for its big trout. It *looks* like big-fish water. We fished it with big streamers and sinking lines and kept our reflexes set at hair trigger. It was one of those days when you figure out fairly soon that you're not going to catch many fish, but maybe you'll get a giant. But the giant didn't come. One of us was always casting from the bow and another from the stern, while the third rowed. Periodically we traded places. We cast and cast. We fished all day without a strike.

Late in the afternoon, on a cast no different than the five hundred that preceded it, to a spot along shore that looked no different than any other spot along shore, I was stripping one of Kelly's Zoo Cougars deep toward the boat in maybe five feet of water when a sizable section of the bottom underwent a sort of seismic shift. I saw motion, a hint of surface disturbance, and then—clearly, with the aid of polarized glasses and an advantageous angle of the sun—the bronze flash of a brown trout turning toward the fly. And I saw dimensions. This was no mere twenty-incher. It was three feet long if it was an inch.

In fishing there is always a risk of diminishing returns. You can set out on a hedonistic course, always searching for larger and more difficult fish and greater and more enduring thrills, but the search can become like the notorious progression from marijuana to heroin. It's possible to get strung out on giant fish and fall victim to the Hemingway syndrome. Hemingway, you remember, abandoned the brook trout of northern Michigan to pursue monster billfish in the Gulf Stream, and his life went downhill from there. It's safest to avoid temptation. Instead of always seeking bigger fish, be satisfied with small ones. Spend most of your time catching ten-inchers on dry flies. They're nice fish, and great fun on light tackle. Be reasonable. You don't need to wrestle giants every day.

But in that two or three seconds, while the biggest brown trout I have ever seen turned and flashed in the Au Sable River, I discovered that I'm not a reasonable man. Not by a long shot.

I didn't catch the trout. Didn't even hook it. At the last moment it turned away, its wariness winning out over the curiosity, hunger, or plain meanness that had spurred it to move. Adrenaline shot from my head to my groin with so much force it felt as if it had been launched from a fire hose. It surged through me, bursting open a window to my core. While the window was open I got a good look inside. There was no mistaking it: I have an addict's heart.

Secret Places

MAYBE, JUST MABYE, IF YOU STRAPPED ME TO A CHAIR with barbed wire, shoved ice picks under my fingernails, set fire to my hair, and crushed my toes one after another with pliers, I'd tell you where I caught that big brown trout last summer. It was in a tangle of drowned logs at the edge of a river in Michigan, I'll say that much. And it took a black Woolly Bugger retrieved fast with a sinking line. I'd be glad to tell you all about it—how the trout charged the fly with the territorial fury of a guard dog trained by the Gestapo and then took off downstream, where it made one wallowing jump and started alligator-rolling on the surface. By the time we got the boat in close, most of my leader was wrapped like butcher's string around the trout. Pat Moore, who was manning the net, kept saying it was a five-pounder, but I'm sure it weighed no more than four pounds, maybe four and a half. We released the fish, and I like to think it's still living beneath the same logjam. I'd be glad to show you how to tie a Woolly Bugger like the one the trout ate. But I won't tell you where he ate it. Sorry.

By nature I'm a generous guy, so I have to work harder than most people to be stingy about my secret fishing spots. To my way of thinking, such discretion is just common sense. In a world growing more crowded by the minute, it's important that we stake out a few places we can call our own.

I once showed my friend James a spot on the upper Manistee where I'd been fishing for years. The river there flows through a parcel of public land almost entirely surrounded by private property, and it can be reached only by following a two-track road through the yard of a man who raises Rottweilers and apparently spends much of his free time shooting rifles at busted washing machines in his yard. Sometimes when you drive past, he stands on his porch in his underwear and watches you. During the sulphur hatch that evening James caught one of the seminal brown trout of his life. It was no giant, only seventeen inches, but it was the biggest trout he had ever caught on a dry fly, and it convinced him that I had led him to a truly epic secret spot. He was so grateful it embarrassed me. He kept giving me boxes of chocolate and cases of imported beer. For weeks he had flowers delivered to my house.

The next season I ran into James one day on that same stretch of water. He was there with his brother-in-law, his accountant, his next-door neighbor, their teenage sons, and ten or twelve Boy Scouts. They had set up a camp of wall tents and picnic tables and were grilling venison burgers when I drove up. James had made friends with the Rottweiler guy, and he was there too. Everybody grinned like crazy and shook my hand. I stayed for a burger, then went home without fishing. I haven't had that stretch to myself since.

The inherent human urge to show off makes it difficult to keep a really good spot from a friend. Unfortunately sharing usually ends up putting a strain on both the spot and the friendship. I fished recently with a retired architect I'll call Ben, who still feels the wounds of a betrayal more than thirty years old. When Ben was a young man he discovered that in late June trout would gather at night in a channel between two lakes not far from his home and feed on *Hexagenia* mayflies. The trout—big ones, fat as defensive linemen—would leave the deep water of the lakes and run into the channel to gorge themselves on bugs. It was a virgin fishery in water everyone assumed was too warm for trout. For years Ben had it to himself.

But the place was so terrific that Ben eventually felt the need to share it with someone. He chose his closest friend, Wayne, who went there and caught a trout so large nobody would have believed it if he hadn't had it mounted by a taxidermist and badgered his wife until she let him hang it in the living room. Wayne would have flossed with hacksaw blades before he told anyone about the spot, but one evening his wife's boss came for dinner and kept standing in front of that mounted monster in the living room saying he would give just about anything to catch a trout like that. By the end of the evening Wayne had had too much wine, and the boss was pestering him to tell him where he'd caught his trout, and his wife was giving him looks that said, *You damned well better cooperate,* so in a fit of generosity he told the guy. He even drew a map. The guy stuck the map in his pocket and smirked. In a voice too low for Wayne's wife to hear, he said, "Sucker."

Wayne's wife's boss went home and called a friend who owned an upscale trout shop in Chicago. The owner of the upscale trout shop came the next night with a group of friends, one of whom was the host of a television fishing show. At dusk the host of the television fishing show caught the biggest trout he had ever seen. Late that night he called his producer and ordered the film crew assembled and sent north at dawn. After the show aired, the river was packed with so many boats filled with flailing anglers that the trout backed down into the lake. They have never returned.

Ben doesn't know who to blame for the loss of his secret spot, so he tends to blame society as a whole. He's now the most secretive of anglers, and frequently bitter. In a recent moment of candor he admitted that he had finally found another place where big trout came in at night during the Hex hatch. He swore that the trout were bigger and more abundant than those at the first spot. Naturally he wouldn't tell me where it was. A few evenings later I tried following him in my car, but he lost me on back roads in Kalkaska County, and now he won't talk to me at all.

It reminds me of something that happened when I was very young. I must have been five years old at the time, because we were living in the Spider House, the dark, cold cottage on the west side of Silver Lake where we spent the winter when I was in first grade. My father had built a fishing shanty and set it on the ice in front of the house. One day he and I were fishing with minnows hooked beneath tip-ups, sitting inside the coop to keep warm until a flag went up, then walking fast across the ice to land the fish. We had caught a large number of walleyes—eight or ten of them, it seems to me now, each as big as a chunk of fireplace wood—and had hidden them in the snow banked around the outside of the coop. The idea was to keep anyone who happened along from knowing how good the fishing was.

As we sat in the dark shanty, somebody crunched across the snow outside and knocked on the door. Dad leaned over and opened it with a fling. A man stood there, silhouetted in blinding light.

"Any luck?" he asked.

Dad answered without hesitation. "Nope. None. None at all."

I was stunned by the enormity of the lie. I had never heard anyone so blatantly disregard the moral lessons Mom had drilled into me. The man stood a moment in silence, then closed the door. He made a slow revolution around the shanty and crunched away into the distance and disappeared.

Neither of us said anything. My father apparently felt no obligation to explain himself. His silence confirmed for me that speaking the truth was required only of children, and probably not even for them when it came to serious matters like fishing and hunting. Better to risk damnation, my father seemed to say, than to give away a good spot to a stranger.

But something about the man's behavior troubled my father. After a few minutes we went outside. There, scattered on the ice around us, were all our lovely frozen walleyes. Somebody's dog had dug them from the snow and spread them out for the world to see.

That day I learned that you must fight to keep your secret spots secret. The world is full of brutal and uncaring people who if given a chance will deceive you and rob you and claim your favorite places as their own. If you treasure your secrets, guard them. Hide them in the attic. Lock them in a vault. Bury them if you must, but deeply, deeply.

Discovering

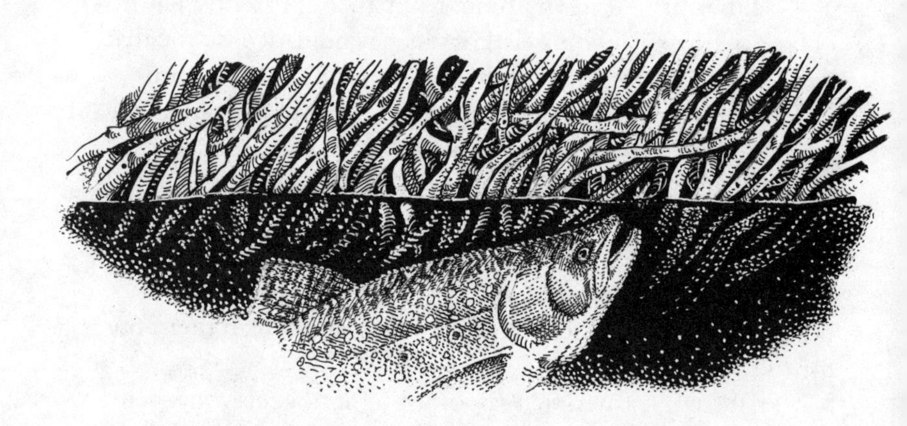

THE FUTURE IS HURTLING TOWARD US, RIPPING UP FORESTS and bridging rivers as it comes, and I have friends who insist I can live with it. They say I should narrow my focus and revise my definition of wilderness. They say I should take a cue from Thoreau and be content to explore a few acres in a lifetime, examining the lives of ants instead of timber wolves, visiting a neighborhood pond instead of a hundred miles of linked lakes in Canada.

Bullshit, I say. I want my world *big*.

But I'm realistic. I don't get to Canada often, so when I discover a creek I've never seen in a swamp thirty miles from home, I try to imagine I'm the first person ever to set foot there. If not the first ever, then the first in years. Or months. Even weeks will do. The idea is to get lost in a place. Get lost, I've learned, and previous visitors become irrelevant.

I discover new places near home with just enough frequency to be heartened. Each time I take a seat in an airplane and fly above nearby counties I see woods I have never hunted, ponds I have never fished, lengths of river that appear—from the air at least—unexplored. I like to think that if my home range were a mansion, there would be entire rooms I have never entered. There would be hidden staircases and a forgotten attic and a bricked-up section of cellar. In the woods next door, screened from the road by trees, would be ponds filled with brook trout.

Last summer I found one of those hidden rooms. I found it because I failed the written test that would license me to be a fishing guide on Michigan's inland waterways. I failed the test because it was spiked with tough multiple-choice questions about Great Lakes marker buoys, and electrical systems on yachts, and the navigation laws involved when maneuvering sailboats in crowded harbors—information I hadn't bothered learning, assuming it would be of no use to a fly-fishing guide rowing a driftboat down the Pere Marquette River. The nice lady behind the counter at the Department of Natural Resources field office invited me to take the test again on the spot and, happily, I passed. That was why I was still there when the chief conservation officer came in from the field.

We had met once several years before, through a mutual friend who spoke highly of him as someone trustworthy. We chatted about the friend and about the places we'd been fishing lately. Then, in what might have been a lapse of good judgment, he mentioned a creek he had been going to in the evenings after work. He said it was remarkable that such a small stream held so many big browns and brookies. Maybe it was the beaver ponds that made it so productive, he said. They stretched down the creek, one following another, most of them firm-bottomed, wadeable, full of cover, and inhabited by good-size trout. He said he knew no stream in Michigan with such prolific hatches of mayflies and caddis. The beaver ponds sometimes churned with rising fish, and he'd lost count of how many sixteen- and seventeen-inchers he'd caught.

Usually when I hear that kind of talk my attention strays. What's the point of listening? Either the stories are exaggerated or they're intended as smoke screens. I nodded politely and thought of all the money I would earn guiding anglers on rivers.

"Here, let me show you," he said and led me to a topographic map laminated to the wall. He searched for a moment, then pointed with the tip of his pencil. "Here it is."

The creek began in swampland and flowed north through the state forest before emptying into a river. Along the way it meandered across a sizable chunk of country I had always bypassed on my way to other places. The conservation officer pointed to the specific bridge where he often began fishing. He said I should feel free to fish there any time. Take a friend if I wanted.

It was humbling. Obviously I was in the presence of a generous spirit. I resolved to somehow return the favor. If the creek panned out, of course.

A few days later Kelly and I were on the stream—let's call it Burke Creek—and, surprise surprise, it was everything it was rumored to be. In fact, it was more.

Getting there was a bit confusing. Our county roads rarely run straight north and south or east and west. They follow the course of least resistance, which means they turn and loop and backtrack through thick upland woods and thick lowland swamps, around moraines and drumlins, down extinct river valleys. Unless the sun is out or you navigate with a compass, it's difficult to keep track of direction. And because the roads are so erratic, most maps tend to blur over the trickiest spots.

Combine that with the road commission's habit of changing the name of a road every time it crosses a county line, plus the likelihood that bored local youths have twisted marker signs ninety degrees, and you need to be patient to find your way around the far corners of my bailiwick. It took a couple of hours—spent pleasantly enough, it's pretty country—but we finally found the bridge and pulled to a stop on top of it and stepped out for a look.

The creek was middling size, about fifteen feet from bank to bank. The upstream side was unpromising, sand bottomed and slightly brown, emerging beneath a wall of alders. While we leaned on the guard rail, we heard crashing in the underbrush and a young man burst into the open. He carried a spinning rod and a canvas creel that appeared suspiciously full. He was surprised to see us on the bridge.

"You guys ever fish here?" he asked.

"Nope."

He shook his head in what could pass for regret and said, "Not much of a creek. Pretty shallow. A few suckers is all."

It was about what I would have said in his situation. Kelly and I walked to the other side of the bridge and leaned over the railing. Below us water poured from a culvert into a waist-deep pool and rollicked over parti-colored cobblestones. *Baetis* spinners bounced above the surface. At the tail of the pool, where the water grew shallow over gravel, a trout splashed.

Not much of a creek.

We climbed into the truck, backtracked to a trail branching north, and drove downstream a mile or two. There we found a turnoff leading toward the creek, took it, descended to low ground, found a spot to park beneath the pines. Five minutes later we were standing thigh deep beneath a canopy of pines and alders, roll-casting tiny Muddlers and catching brook trout every other cast. A couple of hundred yards downstream we came to a beaver pond. It was deep, narrow, cold, with a solid bottom of gravel and with undercut banks along the deep side. It looked like a good home for seventeen-inchers.

I went back three or four times, once during a heavy hatch of blue-winged olives, and caught many trout. None were as big as described by the conservation officer, but they were plump and aggressive and eager to take dry flies. One evening while I stood in one of the ponds trying to get a bead on a rising trout that seemed larger than most, a fawn still in its spots appeared at the edge of the pond, stepped in as daintily as if it were testing the water in a bath, and began swimming toward me. I waited until it was a rod's length away before saying, "Where do you think you're going?" The fawn's eyes grew large. It turned, swam back the way it had come, and disappeared into the brush.

That evening I went exploring. I was curious about the lower end of the creek, where access was more difficult. The farther downstream I went, the better it got. Beaver ponds were separated by stretches of riffles, with deep pools at every bend, and trout in every pool. The end of the creek would turn out to be the best discovery yet.

A BRIEF ASIDE regarding my so-called career as a guide. So far it hasn't worked out. I'm not very good at it. In six trips on the Manistee, Boardman, and Pere Marquette, I barely broke even financially. To equip and protect my clients, I had to buy new rods, reels, lines, coolers, water jugs, rain suits, and other gear. Kelly supplied the drift boat, but by the end of the season I had lost, broken, and replaced two oars and a brass oar-lock. I had also gone through dozens of my own flies, snapped a new graphite rod off at the butt when I jumped out of the boat to help rescue another guide's floundering client, and spent twice as much money as I'd planned on lunches and beverages. Worse, I failed to take my clients to the best places at the best times so they could catch the best trout. I liked the people—they were, without exception, friendly, interesting, and good company, certainly deserving of the best our rivers can offer—but I couldn't bring myself to show them the best places. It's just habit, I suppose. I'm selfish. I cherish solitude. I've practiced deception and trickery so long to protect certain premier spots on my favorite rivers that I couldn't bring myself to betray them for a few hundred bucks a day. I took clients to some pretty good places, but every time I spotted a decent fish I had to wrestle with my demons, which were screaming at me to point the clients in another direction so I could come back the next day and catch the trout myself. I never got comfortable with the role. It was fun helping an Ann Arbor cardiologist's twelve-year-old son catch his first trout on a fly, but it would have been more fun to do it for free. I couldn't get past feeling like the hired help.

In September I guided two doctors on a float for salmon on the Pere Marquette. After lunch, while one doctor tried to snag Chinooks from a pod of restless twenty-pounders, I walked the other upstream to the next pool and started him casting Egg-Sucking Leeches and splitshot on running line, a rig that took his flies quickly to the bottom where they could do the most damage. To his and my considerable surprise, he caught two chrome steelhead, one twenty-nine inches long and the other thirty-two inches. Both took the flies deep in their mouths with aggressive charging strikes. We landed them in spite of the doctor's best efforts to break the leader (he kept clamping down on the reel with both hands when the trout ran) and my best efforts to screw up with the landing net. I had forgotten a camera (a good guide never forgets his camera), so I measured the fish, unhooked them with care, and released them back into the river without giving the doctors anything tangible to show for the experience. I thought the day was a huge success, but the first doctor, who never hooked a fish except for one dorsal-snagged salmon that galloped off downstream until it broke his line, was apparently dissatisfied. I think he expected the outing to be like a charter trip on the Great Lakes and felt cheated because he wasn't going home to his family with a chest cooler filled with slabs of salmon.

I know I'm not good guide material because the best day I had was when a guy from Washington, D.C., hired me for a half-day wade on the Boardman and insisted that I fish along with him. We waded downriver casting streamers and wet flies, chatting as we went, like two fishing buddies. I showed him some good spots, but the trout were uncooperative that day and we caught none over twelve inches. When he wrote me a check at the end of the trip, I was almost ashamed to accept it. He tipped me forty bucks, and I gave him forty bucks' worth of my own flies.

The experience was worthwhile. There were rewards. I got to see the look on that twelve-year-old boy's face, and I found a great steelhead pool on the Pere Marquette. I also discovered a stretch of water on another river that gets terrific spinner falls of *Tricos* on August mornings. The trout were tough, and my client couldn't catch them, but we had fun watching them sip the dinky flies. To appease my demons I went back the next morning on my own and caught several nice fish. I now consider it one of my secret places. Don't even ask.

DISCOVERIES BEGET DISCOVERIES. At its mouth Burke Creek tumbled beneath second-growth pines large enough to pass for virgins, spread across a gravel bar, and spilled into the river. The river itself was the big surprise. Kelly and I knew it well in its upper reaches but had never fished this far downstream. All we knew of the lower water was what we had seen from bridges, where it flowed sluggishly over sand bottom into deep, slow pools we knew the locals fished for walleye and pike. I had canoed it years ago, early in the season, when the river was high and muddy and it all looked the same. I had not been impressed.

Kelly remembers that once a young fisherman stopped in his shop to show him a brown trout he had caught. The trout was stretched out on the back seat of the guy's Jeep Cherokee—no blanket, no plastic bag, just wet trout on unprotected upholstery. But what a trout. Over thirty inches. More than ten pounds. And if Kelly remembers right, the guy told him he caught it during the Hex hatch in one of the walleye holes in the lower river.

The water we saw that day at the creek's mouth flowed quickly over rocks and gravel, with drowned logs along shore and cold springs seeping from the banks: trouty. It looked as good as the blue-ribbon water upstream. Later, checking maps, we noticed that in this same stretch a half dozen creeks dumped their cold water into the river. A hunch started forming.

Kelly, Jerry Wilson, and I floated it a couple of weeks later. We went only a few bends below the put-in before the sluggish water and the frog holes gave way to a riffle. It was fast and deep, with boulders surrounded by churning water and deep gravelly cuts along the banks. A few bends later was another riffle. A mile after that, another.

It was like waking up one morning and finding a trout stream in your basement. We drifted through lovely riffles and rocky pools, in a hardwood valley with few houses and no intermediate access sites. The water was hazy with runoff but clear enough to make our streamers visible from six or eight feet away. And we caught trout. Not many—just three in the first day's float—but all between eighteen and twenty-two inches, including one rowdy rainbow that fought with so much heart that we tipped our hats in respect when we released it. A week later Kelly and I hooked and lost several more trout the same size. In one of the long riffles we happened on a mayfly emergence and caught foot-long rainbows every cast for twenty minutes.

Maybe those two trips were flukes, and we'll never catch another trout there. Further investigation is called for. We want to see how it fishes during the rain. Also during hatches of Hendricksons, Hexes, brown drakes, *Tricos,* and *Epherons.* I'm sure we'll be making discoveries there for years.

We live in a well-explored world, and yes, it seems to be getting smaller. The future is pounding at the door, land is getting gobbled at a terrifying rate, and maybe someday there will no longer be enough space for any of us to be alone. But I keep stumbling across reasons to be hopeful. I've noticed that the planet swells and shrinks depending on how you approach it. On the surface it's small and getting smaller, but the deeper you go, the bigger it gets.

A Trout for the Old Guy

I WAS CLEANING CLOSETS THE OTHER DAY AND CAME ACROSS an old cigar box tucked away in a carton of forgotten fishing gear. I hadn't seen the box in decades, but it gave off the aura of something once familiar and cherished, and I knew immediately what it contained: dry flies tied by an old man I had not seen, had hardly even thought about, for nearly twenty-five years. I remembered the flies as if I had placed them in the closet just the day before. And I remembered the old man as if we had fished together last week—as if I were still an overeager kid of seventeen and he a venerable regular on the Boardman River.

I met him on a May afternoon when I had driven to the

river after school to fish the afternoon hatches. We didn't actually meet, in the formal sense. I would see him many times that summer, but I never asked his name and he never offered it. I began to think of him simply as the old guy.

It had been a warm spring, every day so bright and lovely it could have been July. That afternoon I found a good trout rising above Brown Bridge and waded out by the twin culverts, where the river flowed deep and smooth before slipping into darkness beneath the bridge. When cars passed, dust billowed in little storms above the gravel and coated all the trees along the road with a layer of khaki.

Across the river, where the water was deepest and shaded by leaning cedars, the same trout fed regularly, each abrupt rise leaving a ring and a bubble drifting downstream into the culvert. I knew by the determined cadence of its feeding that this trout could be caught, but every time I attempted to cast, I got tangled in the branches of the cedars leaning above it or broke off my fly in the alders behind me. Finally I grew frustrated and quit.

I turned to wade back to the bridge. An old man was leaning against the guardrail above, watching. He was sixty or seventy or eighty, I couldn't tell. At seventeen any age over forty seemed ancient to me.

"Want to try for him?" I asked.

"I wouldn't mind."

He came down the bank, stepped past me into the water, and shook some line loose from his rod. It was bamboo, colored the rich glossy brown of freshly baked bread. He wore old canvas waders and a felt hat with a single streamer stuck in the band. His face showed decades.

He roll-cast to lift his line, flicked it back, flicked it forward, and the fly touched the water beneath the cedars and rode downstream high on its hackles. The trout took it with a determined grab, jumped, and made a few circular dashes in the pool. Then the old man led it into the shallows at our feet. A brown trout, maybe a foot long.

"Pretty fish," he said. He palmed it, unhooked it, and steadied it in the current until it swam off. "You false-cast too much, young man. Don't use so much effort. And you need a lighter line for that rod."

Then he waded slowly up the edge of the river and disappeared around the bend.

We saw each other regularly after that. Sometimes we spoke, but usually not. He never greeted me unless I greeted him first, and I never saw him smile. When he was in the river, I often stopped on the bank a courteous distance away and watched. His casts were always short and accurate. He would cast, wade forward a few steps, make a single crisp backcast, and cast again. No wasted motion. I never saw him raise a large trout, but I watched him land many small ones, and I was convinced that he caught big sophisticated browns when I wasn't around. He seemed to fish only with dry flies. I wanted to be just like him.

It was obvious that he didn't want a friend, but I was starved for instruction and convinced he could educate me. I had grown up in an atmosphere in which learning was prized; it never occurred to me that I would be refused. I assumed that all I had to do was figure out the right way to ask.

One Saturday I caught him sitting on the bank smoking a cigar, his rod across his knees. It seemed proper to join him.

He grunted when I said hello and shrugged when I asked if he had caught anything. He made no response at all when I told him that I had caught a couple of ten-inchers.

It was a lie. I had caught nothing.

I opened my fly box and told him he was welcome to examine the contents. He looked at me so long that I began to squirm like a grade-school ruffian.

"Do you want something from me, young man?"

"Yes sir."

"Spit it out then."

"What's the best way to catch a five-pound brown trout in this river? And where?"

"A five-pound brown trout."

"Yes sir."

"Four pounds won't do?"

"That would be okay, too."

"I'd recommend dynamite. Below Sabin Dam."

"In the deep water below the powerhouse?"

"And in the first bend downstream."

"Will they take flies?"

"Dynamite's better, but yes, on rare occasions, if you're skillful and lucky, they'll take a fly."

Then I confessed that I had not caught a pair of ten-inchers, that, to be honest, a lot of days I failed to catch a single fish, and that, in fact, my total experience with trout a foot or more in length was limited to a few heavy tugs on wet flies in deep water and a single (but plump!) fourteen-incher that charged across a dozen feet of flat water to wallop a Muddler I was yanking around on the surface because I was bored.

He must have felt some sympathy. Or maybe he just wanted to get rid of me. "Tomorrow morning, ten o'clock, below Sabin. Park at the dam and walk downstream on the right bank about a quarter mile until you come to an old shack made of cement blocks. I'll try to meet you there. If I don't show up, don't let it ruin your day. Now get the hell out of here, and let me finish my cigar in peace."

AT DAWN THE next morning, I was casting streamers into the roiling water below the discharge pipes at Sabin Dam. I caught nothing there, so I tried the riffles downstream and the pool on the outside of the first bend. Finally, with hours to kill before ten o'clock, I reeled in and went exploring.

I followed a trail around the first bend and came to a creek that wound down from the hills and emptied into the river. It was cold and clear—brook trout water. I had been fishing such creeks for years, fishing them the way my father taught me and his father taught him, with nightcrawlers and garden worms threaded on wire hooks. At its lower end, near the river, the creek shimmied out of sight beneath tangles of alders. I followed it upstream, to higher ground, where the alders gave way to cedars and there was room to fish.

I had recently read an article in a sporting magazine about fly-fishing small streams using a technique called dapping, which involves lowering a fly on a short leader until it touches the surface of the water, then raising and lowering it to make it look like a dancing insect. Trout could not resist it, the author said. They would jump all over themselves to get at the fly.

I bellied up to within a rod's length of a pool where the creek plunged over a log, and, lowering a fly to the water, I dapped away. Nothing. I moved upstream to the next pool. Nothing there either.

Changing flies didn't help. Maybe it was the creek. Maybe it held no trout at all.

I walked off into the woods and kicked over logs until I found a half dozen earthworms. With my pocketknife I stripped the hackle and fur from a badly used fly and tied the bare hook to my leader, then baited it with a worm, pinched on a splitshot, and lowered the bait into a pool. A brook trout darted out of the foam and smacked it. I lowered it again, and another trout came. Every spot that looked like it should hold a trout did. Most were only six or eight inches long, but a few reached ten. I kept a couple of the biggest, killing them and slipping them into the pocket in the back of my vest.

A half mile above the river the brook grew shallow over a long stretch of gravel, and I walked quickly along the bank to get to more promising water. I was thinking cheerful thoughts about nothing in particular and was almost past the gravel stretch when I saw movement in the creek ahead of me. There, beside the bank, partly obscured by grass hanging over the water, were the flank and wide tail of a trout. A very large trout.

It was too big for a brookie—too big for any fish that lived in such small water. It had to be a steelhead. Sometimes when they run up rivers to spawn, they keep going and get into small tributaries. This one seemed not to know its own size. The grassy bank under which it tried to hide covered only half its body.

I stripped line from my reel and lobbed the worm into the creek two or three feet above the fish. It was a gesture, like tossing off a shot at a grouse when it's already sixty yards away and banking past a spruce. You don't expect to hit the bird. And you don't expect a steelhead to take a worm.

But this one did. It charged forward and flared its gill covers and inhaled the worm almost before it reached bottom.

I had no chance of landing it. The trout was too big, the creek too small, and I was using a light rod rigged for brook trout. All the steelhead had to do was turn downstream and accelerate and my leader would have popped.

Instead it panicked. It gave a powerful sweeping thrust of its tail, threw water four feet in the air, and shot straight across the creek and out of the water onto a bed of gravel. It was still bouncing when I got to it. I pinned it to the ground with my hands and knees.

It was a bright female, with a blush of red on the gill covers and a faint pink stripe down the side. I lifted it and admired its sleek, muscular heft and thick shoulders, its sides gleaming like metal just trimmed on a lathe. Later, when my father and I hung it on the scale in our garage, we would find that it weighed a little over seven pounds.

Today I would release such a fish immediately. But this was a long time ago, and I was very young. I killed it with a blow to the head.

My watch showed almost ten o'clock. I slid my fingers beneath the gill plate and carried the fish downstream toward the river. After a few steps I stopped and laid it on the ground. I clipped the bare hook from my leader and took out my fly box. Inside was a good-looking Adams that had fooled a few small trout in the river. I tied it on, stuck it in the cork handle of my rod, and drew the line tight. Then I picked up the steelhead and went looking for the old guy.

I DIDN'T FIND him. He never showed. I saw him a few days later and many other days that summer, but he wouldn't talk to me. If he saw me coming, he went the other way or became suddenly very busy tying on a tippet or a fly. If I waved, he pretended not to notice. I wondered if I had done something wrong, and because I could not imagine what, I became angry.

We didn't speak again until after school started in September and the maples were turning colors. One Saturday I answered a classified ad in the newspaper—"Trout flies, reasonable"—and was given an address on the phone. I drove to a house on Arbutus Lake and knocked on the door. The old guy answered. I hardly recognized him. He was bald and wore a cardigan sweater. Without his hat and waders he seemed smaller.

"It's you," he said. He opened the door for me to step inside but didn't invite me farther into the house. We faced each other in the foyer. I asked how the fishing had been. He said he had not been out much the last few weeks. Then he told me that his wife was sick, had been sick since last winter, and they had been trying to sell the house for months. Now it was sold, and in two weeks they would be in Arizona. For her health, he said. Before they moved he had to get rid of some things he no longer needed.

For twelve dollars he sold me a White Owl cigar box

containing four dozen dry flies, heaped in a mound like a wren's nest, and two small bottles of dry-fly floatant he and a friend had invented and marketed many years earlier. The floatant was laced with aquatic insects that had been chopped up and stirred into a paraffin solution. "The insects give it a natural scent," he said. It worked well enough, but it hadn't sold. There seemed to be nothing left to say after that, so I gave him my money and took the flies and the bottles of floatant and left. I never saw him again.

That's what I remembered while standing in the closet, examining the flies still in the cigar box. There weren't many left, and something had eaten most of the hackle, but you could still see the care that had gone into tying those Adamses, Cahills, and Pale Morning Duns. The bottles of floatant were gone. I had used them for two or three seasons, and they had worked very well indeed.

I'm old enough now to realize what a nuisance I must have been to the old man, and to be sorry for it. He obviously wanted only to be alone in his last season on the river; he hadn't needed the company of a brash and zealous seventeen-year-old obsessed with glory and other things foolish and fleeting.

But I had been too young to know that—too young to understand the ways of rivers and time. Too damned young to know a breaking heart when I saw one.

"Simplify, Simplify"

I DREAMED OF LIVING ALONE, IN THE WOODS, MILES FROM ANY neighbor, in a house I built myself beside a crackerjack trout stream where I had all the time I wanted to fish and hunt and loaf around and could earn a good living without working very hard. But the land along crackerjack trout streams costs more than I can afford, so I live in an old farmhouse across the road from a thriving subdivision and I work all the time. Or nearly all the time. The trout streams are twenty or thirty miles away, and I drive to them several times a week. The remainder of my waking hours I spend as a sojourner in civilized life and try not to whine about it.

I am determined to live deliberately. I refuse to fritter my life away on details. Even in this age of telecommunications and superhighways it is possible to live a simple life, a life of contemplation and serenity. The choppy seas of civilized life still hold pockets of calm.

Consider a typical day at my house, say in March, when winter lingers but the days grow long and bright. Gail and the boys rise early, at the crack of dawn, that hour of genius; I, a nocturnal bird who often works all night, rise at nine. I make coffee, read the newspaper over breakfast, amble up to my office by ten or so. I work until noon, and, if I feel like it, drive into town to the library or to meet friends for lunch—although these days Gail often needs the truck to get to her own job, which began as one day a week assisting a friend at her commercial art studio and has escalated to three days a week and a promotion to project manager and designer. Aaron usually needs the car to drive to school and, afterward, to go to work at the neighborhood supermarket or play basketball or roller hockey or be with his girlfriend. More often than not, I'm stranded here.

No matter. I make a sandwich and work while I eat. I work all afternoon (although days when Gail works, I quit early to make dinner, and while it's cooking throw a load of laundry in the washer and maybe yank the vacuum across the living room carpet) and meet Nick at the door when he gets dropped off by the bus and comes prancing into the house in his usual good spirits. He tells me about his day, and, more often than not, runs out again to go to his buddy Danny's house across the field. Or Danny comes here. Or Jeff or Eric or Hayden comes over. Or there's something going on at school—sports, usually, though soccer and track won't start until the weather breaks in April—and I'll get on the phone with the parents of Nick's friends and we'll figure out rides going and back, and snacks (dinner won't be until 6:30, and the boys need to graze hourly), and compare notes on homework to make sure no assignments have been forgotten or lost.

Gail comes home, then Aaron, and we set the table for dinner, unless the table is piled with books or the freshly glued parts of a scale model of the Challenger space shuttle, in which case we eat on trays in the living room with the news on. After dinner we flip a coin, and one of us does dishes and the other jump-starts Nick with his homework and Aaron goes upstairs to his bedroom where he can listen to Rage Against the Machine as loud as he wants while he attends to his own homework. Once the kids are occupied, Gail and I work out in the basement (light stuff—dumbbells and stationary bike) or, if the weather is nice and the roads clear, go for a walk. Then it's off to the library or to a meeting or to the supermarket. We begin nudging Nick toward bed at nine so he'll be there by ten; then Gail and I sit on the couch for a few minutes to plan the next day. She goes to bed and reads. I stay up and read or tie flies or watch basketball or hockey on television or, if it absolutely can't be avoided, work. Every week or two we go to a movie or join friends for dinner. Holidays we spend with our parents and brothers and sisters. If I can get away, I fish the Platte or the Pere Marquette for steelhead. Honey, I'm going fishing. See ya!

MODERN LIFE IS simple. A piece of cake. There's nothing to it. We have more free time than we know what to do with. We possess so many modern conveniences that we buy computers just to monitor them. With a little planning and organization, the days slip smoothly by. Who says family life is hectic?

Sure, it can get a little hectic in the summer, when school's out and Gail gets called to work on her day off and Toby, the puppy, who is not yet housebroken, requires watching every waking moment, and Aaron, Nick, and Toby keep coming to my office door complaining that there's nothing in the house to eat. On days like that it's possible for our carefully maintained equilibrium to be bumped out of kilter. Some household item breaks—the toaster, say, or the lamp hanging over the dining room table, which is always being clobbered by hockey sticks and tennis balls—or somebody comes down with a cold; or the power goes out, erasing a day's worth of work on my computer; or the septic system backs up; or a bluejay slams into the front window and needs to be brought inside and made comfortable in a shoebox with a lightbulb for warmth and fed a puree of earthworms and milk until it dies; or second cousins from Toledo show up unannounced and we convert the living room into a guest room and start cooking for ten; or a telemarketer calls while I'm blotting puppy urine from the carpet with a dish towel in one hand and the portable phone in the other and potatoes are boiling over on the stove and Nick is in the bathroom shouting that we're out of toilet paper and the puppy is under the couch chewing on Aaron's hundred-dollar Nikes and somebody is pounding on the door and the smoke alarm goes off. Then, sure, it gets a little hectic, but we can handle it. It helps to think of Thoreau. "Simplify, simplify," he wrote. "Why should we live with such hurry and waste of life?"

I remember the night Glenn Wolff and I walked half drunk in the rain through the subdivision where his friends Kathleen and Alfred live in Concord, Massachusetts. We put on raincoats and followed Alfred across his neighbor's yard, cut through a fringe of trees, and sprinted between cars across the highway and somehow made our way through the dark woods with a flashlight that kept blinking out and found the foundation of the old cabin next to Walden Pond. We stepped inside the cables strung around the perimeter of the site and located the ancient hearthstone and read its inscription by flashlight: "Go thou my incense upward from my hearth." We experienced what I guess could be called an epiphany when we walked the path Thoreau wore from his door to the pondside and stood on the beach where he must have stood a hundred nights looking across that black water, wondering what the hell he was doing there.

The suspicion creeps in that modern life is not so simple after all. It was not very simple even in Henry's day, but at least he and his neighbors were never bothered by telemarketers. I listen to a young woman reciting in a sexless voice the news that I have been selected from a list of unusually intelligent consumers to take advantage of a special offer for high-quality lifetime-guaranteed vinyl siding that can be installed at an unbelievably low price (if I act now) and will raise the value of my house thousands of dollars—and when she pauses for breath I say that my house is already beautifully sided, thank you, and now it's mahogany-dun time on the Manistee.

See ya!

I WORK HARD these June days, rising by the crack of nine and going upstairs to my cluttered office—that den of missed deadlines—to call editors and explain that overdue articles will be finished and in their hands no later than a week from next Tuesday. I log a few hours on the computer, then play solitaire until the mail comes. Afternoons I excise excess words and answer the mail. Evenings I cut and nail fascia to cover the ragged raftertails of our house, and wear a carpenter's apron for my wife's enjoyment. Last week her parents parked their motor home in our yard and immediately began painting our house. It's a big job, and I'll always be grateful to them, but their activity stirred ambition, even in me. I dusted off the circular saw and started carpentering.

Soon I realized my folly. The house got along without fascia for 125 years, so who am I to meddle with it now? If God had wanted this house finished, wouldn't he have made some other fool do it? But such reasoning goes unheeded in these secular times. Besides, a responsible adult never leaves a job undone. Never. No matter what. Not even when the days are overcast and sultry and the brown drakes are hatching. Not even when Kelly calls to say that Ray had a huge day yesterday below Hodenpyle: two rainbows over twenty-seven. Kelly's floating it in the morning. Want to go? Yes, yes, of course. But I have sentences to cut and nail, one-by-sixes to compose and polish. A responsible adult never abandons a distasteful and difficult job, even one that might run contrary to divine plan, to go fishing with his buddies on a lovely stretch of wild river and perhaps catch the trout of the decade.

Six o'clock? At the shop? Damn right.

See ya!

I DON'T KNOW why I need to fish so much. For the good of my soul? The question makes me skittish. I prefer to think of fishing as a restorative to some vital thing—maybe soul, maybe heart, maybe vitality itself—that dwindles when we spend too much time working, attending to family and fiscal emergencies, driving in traffic, and watching television. I don't know much about the soul, but I know that the twin benefits of fishing—the combination of physical activity with cerebral engagement—serve to flush impurities from my system. When I haven't been out for a few days I suffer from a buildup of hideous poisons. My joints ache. My muscles cramp. My fingernails get brittle. If I sleep, I dream of forest fires and exploding trains. Tears stream down my cheeks, leaving trails of toxic salts. I pace the floor and sigh until Gail kicks me out of the house, which is all I needed in the first place.

Once a few years ago it got so bad that I decided to throw a sleeping bag and a fly rod into the car and drive across the continent in search of the river with the loveliest name I could find. Call it a quest for the correlation between superficial and intrinsic beauty. I wanted a hands-on study of rivers.

But vehicle number one was in the shop with a faulty transmission and would not be available for a week. It ran great, but only in first gear. Estimate: five hundred to a thousand dollars. Then, checking vehicle number two, I discovered why the radiator fluid had been disappearing. The dipstick came out looking like a straw pulled from a double-chocolate milkshake. The same mechanic—his eyes get bright when he sees me now—said it meant a blown head gasket or a warped head or a cracked block or all three. Estimate: three hundred dollars to infinity. We were careless. Foiled in my quest, facing unattractive choices, I did what any sensible person would do.

Yo, Kelly, wanna float the Pine? Can you pick me up?

See ya!

I DREAMED OF a house without a lawn, where the leaves that fell every fall were still there in the spring, where wind was the only rake I owned and frost the only Weed-Whacker. Instead I live on an acre of grass surrounded by a dozen slovenly gardens shaded by trees so profligate they could bury me with their leaves. Autumn Saturdays I rake. Summer Saturdays I mow. I mow and I mow and I mow. Aaron, about to disembark for college, says mowing ruined his adolescence and makes himself scarce. Nick, at ten, can mow the flat front yard, but he is too small yet for hills, and most of the lawn is hills. So until he grows, I mow. Saturdays are not mine. After lunch I begin mowing, and at dinner I am still mowing. Good weather is the enemy. It does horrible things to grass. I would let it grow, permit it to follow its natural course, but others in the family have a strong prejudice against nature's plan. So while the sun shines, I mow.

But today is cloudy! The sky glowers with dark clouds! At noon the mower is gassed and poised in the garage, but I would not subject it to damaging moisture. Then it is raining, a slow steady shower that blackens the bark on the trees and bends the leaves of grass and suspends a silver drop from each, like a tear. The sky descends and the wind dies. The road sheens darkly, and suddenly the air above it is filled with mayfly spinners. Thousands of them rise and fall in a mating orgy. I bag a couple in my hat and note that they are bigger than brown drakes, smaller than *Hexagenia*. No doubt they are one of the lake species I know nothing about; they must have emerged last night from the bay and hidden all day in trees along shore. Now they've been tricked by the dark sky into flying and have mistaken the wet road for water. All their lives they prepared for this moment, only to spill their eggs uselessly on asphalt. The air is filled with futility. I'm witness to a lost generation.

But if mayflies are mating above the road, surely they are mating above the river. The day is young, and the lawn is too wet to mow. My rod, my vest, my waders.

See ya!

SIMPLIFY, SIMPLIFY. THE fascia is finished, and all but one side of the house is painted. In August the lawn needs mowing only on second Saturdays, in September not even that, and in October, with luck, the wind will blow most of the leaves to the neighbor's yard. On summer nights like this, if I mute the television and turn off the CD player and if there are no parties in the subdivision and the Coast Guard isn't practicing night rescues over the bay with their helicopter and no kids race cars up Blue Water Road and the phone doesn't ring, I can hear waves from the living room. I sit with my head to the screen, listening. It's the same sound Glenn and I heard that rainy night at Walden Pond, the sound of the world's secret cadence, a whispered promise that everything will pass and all is well. Simplify, simplify. The puppy is sleeping, the kids are playing Nintendo in their bedroom, Gail is reading a novel and emanating waves of contentment. If I am not living quite the life I dreamed, so what? It's a good life, a full life, made bright with love and light and laughter.

Saint Henry said that the sun is but a morning star, but I've never figured out exactly what he meant by that. He also said that a living dog is better than a dead lion, which sounds insulting at first but isn't a bad sentiment once you get used to it. I would rephrase his most famous line: The mass of dogs lead lives of quiet desperation. But not this dog. No sir. This dog is going fishing in the morning.

See ya!

Fish Naked

NAKED WE COME INTO THE WORLD AND NAKED WE LEAVE it, but deciding what to wear in the meantime can be a pain in the duff. I consider shopping for clothes about as much fun as shingling condominiums, so I like to wear the same blue jeans and corduroy shirt most days, and would probably wear them *every* day if my wife and kids didn't complain. I'm not lazy or undisciplined or unclean, just uninterested.

But when I was in my early twenties, my fishing friends and I were fashion paragons, on the cutting edge of what would eventually become known as the grunge look. We grew our hair long (and yes, Dad, you were right: Someday we *did* look back at the photos and cringe) and dressed only in jeans, tees, and flannel shirts. Because we were too obsessed with fishing and hunting to land good jobs, money was scarce. It condemned us to sleeping in our cars when we traveled and fishing with cheap waders, mid-range fiberglass rods, and decent but not great Hardy reels. We filled mismatched plastic boxes with flies we tied ourselves and stuffed them inside vests so stained with sweat and blood and spilled dry-fly floatant they looked as if they'd been kicked around on the floor of an automobile repair shop that doubled as a slaughterhouse.

For a few years in the mid-seventies, Mike McCumby and I drove west every September to fish the waters in and around Yellowstone Park, a region that even then was a center of outdoor fashion. Mike and I stood out from the rest of the crowd. When we entered fly shops the proprietors looked at us the way a famously conservative congressman from northern Michigan looked at hippies—as road dreck that arrived in town with one pair of underwear and one five-dollar bill and no intention of changing either of them. Mike and I weren't hippies, but neither were we in the market for Wheatley fly boxes or a hundred-dollars' worth of Japanese-tied Humpies and Bitch-Creek Nymphs. To get useful information we had to spring for a couple spools of tippet material and endure the head-to-foot glances of customers who wore more money on their backs than Mike and I earned in two weeks of pounding nails. Screw 'em, we said. Our outfits sucked, but man, we *fished.*

One year we spent every day for a week on the Firehole. We concentrated on the meadow sections of the river, in the midst of geyser fields, mud pots, and boiling streams. It's hard to imagine water more unlike the staid, cedar-shrouded rivers we had grown up fishing back home in Michigan. We became a bit delirious with the novelty of casting where there were few trees to snag our backcasts and where large fish fed recklessly on the surface in midstream, at midday.

The Firehole's trout see a lot of skillfully presented artificial flies and can be fussy about which ones they eat. Mike and I did okay, fooling a few good fish every afternoon during mayfly hatches and taking rainbows and browns to eighteen inches on weighted nymphs dead-drifted through some of the deeper riffles. That was during working hours, when we had much of the river to ourselves. On the weekend we had to share.

We knew the Firehole was popular, but we were not prepared for the crowds that gathered at every bend and riffle that bright September Saturday. Much of the competition was composed of deeply intent young men and women who dressed as if they had been assisted by personal fashion consultants and cast as if they had been tutored from the crib by tournament champs. Mike and I were a little intimidated. On previous trips to less fashionable places in Wyoming and Montana, we had shared the water with locals wading wet in dusty blue jeans and cowboy hats, carrying Band-Aid boxes of flies in their shirt pockets, and casting heavy glass rods with most of the paint chipped off. They were after-work anglers, good at muscling Woolly Worms into the wind and keeping their freezers stocked. Although Mike and I considered them kindred spirits, they dismissed us as effete fancy-pants purists because we wore chestwaders with only a few patches on them and preferred long leaders and smallish dry flies over the giant, gaudy, subaquatic patterns that were standard in most Western fly boxes in those days. One afternoon on the Madison an elderly cowboy casting large nineteenth-century-style wet flies on snelled hooks laughed out loud when we told him we were using #20 Blue-Winged Olives and 6X tippets. Later, surrendering to the when-in-Rome principle, we ambushed the Madison with Spruce Flies the size of neotropical songbirds and caught just as many fish as we were accustomed to catching, but they averaged half a foot longer.

On the Firehole we kept running into expert midgers casting thousand-dollar rods and wearing outfits like the folks in the Orvis catalog. They looked us up and down in frank appraisal, bent over to read the logos on our rods and reels, and more often than not began furiously dropping names. "I fished this stretch once with Ernest," one yawning dude said, sliding up to Mike and me on the bank of a drop-dead pool where a few minutes earlier we had watched a brown trout big enough to eat a muskrat rise, just once, during a brief hatch of minuscule gray somethings. The dude didn't specify which Ernest he meant, and we were too polite to ask. Then, later, while Mike worked a gravel run downstream and I stood on a rock casting dry flies and watching a streamside geyser erupt, a meticulously dressed gentleman with a cosmetic suntan walked to within twenty feet of me and began casting into the same pool. As I reeled in he leaned my way and said, "I helped Jack Hemingway land and release a twenty-eight-inch brown trout from that exact spot a month ago."

Well, I was glad to hear it. I've always wanted to catch a twenty-eight-inch brown trout, and any rumor of one's existence is encouraging. But I had seen enough superbly dressed, superbly equipped, and superbly connected fishermen for one day, so I excused myself and rounded up Mike and we hiked through a stand of lodgepole pines to intercept the river in an area the map showed was as far from roads and boardwalks as any stretch of the Firehole gets. It was a hot day, grasshopper weather, and we walked a fair distance. We were sweating like wrestlers when we finally spotted sunlight flashing on water through the trees.

But then we saw the glint of a rod and stopped. Pilgrims were everywhere on this holy water. We were pilgrims too, of course, but after fishing an uncrowded river all week it was hard to be charitable. We walked to the edge of the woods to see what we were up against.

Facing us from the shallows on the opposite bank was a powerfully built man wearing skin-tight, skin-toned waders, with a landing net hanging below his waist and a fly rod waving around his head. Two heartbeats later, in a kind of cognitive double-take, I realized that the man was wearing neither waders nor clothes. He was stitchless, buck-naked, bare-assed as a baby. And there is no delicate way to say this: That thing hanging to his knees was no landing net. The guy was a freak of nature. P. T. Barnum could have made a fortune off him.

Mike and I drew back into the woods and hunkered down to think. We stayed quiet, not wanting to alert the guy to our presence. It sounds strange now, but we were spooked. Seeing a naked man fishing is odd enough, but this naked man brought to mind the biological concept of dominance hierarchy. We were six-point bucks intruding on a twelve-pointer's territory, and we sure as hell didn't want him to think we were challenging him for it.

"Did you see that?" Mike whispered.

"I'm not sure," I said. "You're talking about the nude guy in the river?"

"Yea. But did you see *that*?"

We stepped to the edge of the trees. The man was gone. In his place was a woman, knee deep in the river, placing short, splashy casts to midstream. She too was starkers. And her physique was just as extraordinary as the man's. She had the kind of body that is considered out of fashion nowadays but can be seen on glorious display in Greek statuary, saucy Renaissance paintings, and turn-of-the-century French postcards. Venus with a fly rod.

Now we were really spooked. Where was the man? And what would he do if he caught us spying on his girlfriend? We cut through the woods, taking frequent glances behind us, and came out on the river a long bend downstream, in open terrain, where we could keep an eye on the woman above us and see anyone approaching when they were still a hundred yards away. But now the naked woman and the naked man were together, standing side by side and casting in synchronized rhythm, like the original innocent anglers of Eden. If Mike and

I had been first-time visitors to the planet, we might have assumed we were witnessing some form of ritual courtship display.

We had a stretch of river to ourselves, at least, so we took our time and fished carefully. A middle-aged man wearing tight waders and a slouch hat furred with dozens of flies passed us on the bank and gave a jolly hello. We returned his greeting and watched him walk upstream to the bend where Adam and Eve fished. He stopped beside them and exchanged words as if there were nothing unusual about encountering naked people on the Firehole. It was disorienting. Mike and I wondered if we were terribly misinformed. Maybe nude angling was a local tradition, promoted by the West Yellowstone Chamber of Commerce and celebrated with effusive prose in travel magazines. Maybe it was a *tactic.*

We cast nymphs for an hour or so, but the trout seemed to have hightailed it to the headwaters. No insects were hatching, and the river was shallow and empty of life. All the time we fished we watched the man and woman. They never raised a trout. If nudity was a tactic, it didn't work.

It occurred to us that we might be witnessing a fashion statement. Maybe the nudists were protesting designer labels and de rigueur fishing duds, casting off all superfluities and announcing bravely to the world that only the river and the fishing mattered. The idea was nice, but it probably didn't apply. My guess is it just felt good to take your clothes off and stand in the water and show off a little. Mike and I laughed about it as we made our way downstream. For the first time all week we were the best-dressed guys on the river.

Tying Your Own

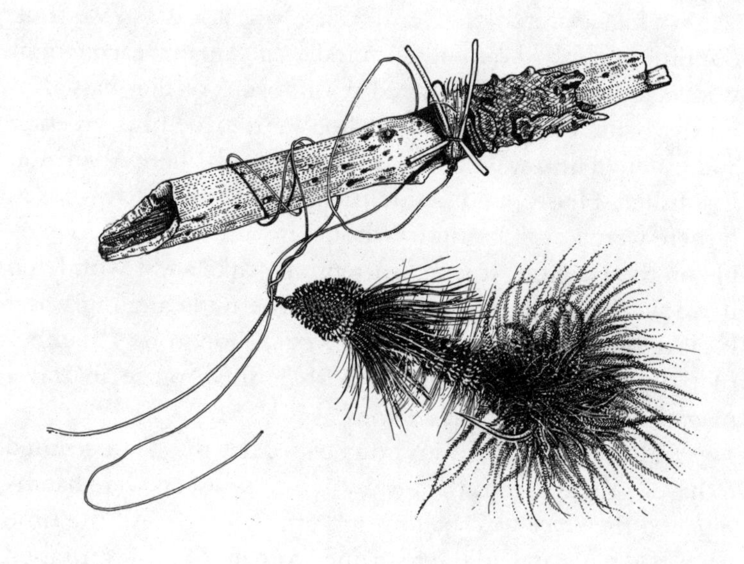

IN MY TEENS AND TWENTIES I IMAGINED MIDDLE AGE AS A TIME when I would spend winter evenings tying flies by a fireplace, snowflakes beating soundlessly against the windows, tasteful music playing in the background. Now, at the middling age of forty-two, I've achieved an approximate version of that. This evening I'm tying elk-hair caddis, the fire is lit, snowflakes are falling, and in the background are Nick and his friends shouting over the repetitive blaring sounds of John Madden's NFL Football on the Nintendo. Not exactly music, but close enough.

Every winter I set out to tie enough flies to last through the following season. I'm not very disciplined, so it takes determination to sit at the desk and whip up a season's worth of Adams dry flies, for instance, a dozen each in sizes 14, 16, and 18, and an equal number of parachute Adamses. That's a lot of Adamses, especially at the rate I tie, and invariably before I'm through with the size 14s my mind is wandering to other patterns. Next thing I know the fly I'm working on is finished, it's a little uglier than I had hoped it would be, and I'm pulling deer hair and turkey feathers from the drawer and making a Muddler Minnow because I just remembered a nice brown trout that streaked up from a pool in the Carp a few years ago and smacked one. It was the same evening, come to think of it, that an Adams did so well for rainbows in that river's rapids. I was standing on a high bank, ten feet above the water, and saw the trout rush the fly but miss. I cast again, and the trout came up again and swirled behind the Muddler. I gathered my breath (this was a nice trout) and cast a third time. He struck. I struck. Eighteen inches, and so big around he must have spent his days pigging out on kielbasa and beer. A guy can never have too many Muddlers.

Tying your own flies is immensely satisfying, and I'm convinced it can make you a better angler, not only because it makes it easier to keep your fly boxes stocked, but also because it stimulates innovation and trains you to be more attentive to aquatic life. It might even make you a better person, in the sense that performing small, tedious acts forces you to slow down, which can help you to become more observant in the way Henry James meant when he advocated being someone who misses nothing. If you can notice that a mayfly has three tails instead of two, you might also notice when a crisis is building at home. Maybe not. But it can't hurt.

Most fly tiers I know began out of economic necessity. Artificial flies are as expendable as Dixie cups, yet they're expensive. If you fish with light tippet on small, overgrown rivers, you can easily lose a dozen flies in a couple of hours. At two or three dollars each, it can get expensive. So we tie our own to save money. Or we justify it by saying we save money. I'm not sure we do. A good tying vise, a rooster neck loaded with dry-fly hackle, and a basic assortment of furs, feathers, threads, tinsels, hooks, scissors, hackle pliers, head cement, and bobbins adds up to a considerable investment. That's just to get started. It can become as expensive as gourmet cooking.

The comparison is instructive. A serious amateur cook and a serious amateur fly tier have much in common. Both are intensely interested in utensils and ingredients. Both linger over exotic, high-priced products displayed in specialty shops. Both subscribe to magazines devoted to their interests and pore over every issue. Both rush to purchase the latest four-color hardbound book of recipes—"patterns" in fly-tying jargon—each recipe and pattern accompanied by an itemized list of ingredients, precise step-by-step instructions, and a luscious close-up photograph of the finished product. The photos in both cookbooks and fly-tying manuals are calculated to inspire.

When fly-tying friends get together and start comparing patterns, the conversation can get downright mouthwatering. One evening Doug Stanton and his wife, Anne, invited Gail and me to their house for dinner. For starters they served medallions of venison tenderloin, roasted green peppers, and blue cheese spread on a fresh baguette. The main course was grilled woodcock (served very rare), sautéed grouse breast, roasted garlic, mashed potatoes with garlic, and candied baby carrots. We drank an inexpensive merlot with dinner and, for dessert, snifters of Calvados. Splendid! After the meal, Doug and I pulled out our fly boxes and I gave him my recipe for Hendricksons. Here it is:

One size-14 Tiemco TMC 100 hook
One spool 8/0 prewaxed olive thread
Six or eight stiff fibers from a blue-dun hackle
(or substitute dark-dun Microfibetts)
Clump of bronze Hi-Vis

One grade 1 or 2 Hoffman blue-dun rooster hackle
Pinch of dubbing fur
Dash of head cement
1/4 tsp. garlic butter

Attach blue-dun hackle fibers at bend of hook for tail, extending about the length of the hook, and split into a V of about 45 degrees. Wrap thread to eye of hook, and lash in a single upright wing of bronze Hi-Vis.

Make body of dubbing fur consisting of one-third muskrat (guard hairs removed), one-third olive Superfine Dubbing, and one-third cinnamon Superfine. Blend the dubbing, picking and mixing to an even consistency (but don't overblend, or it will turn a homogeneous brown), and spin from bend of the hook to front of wing, starting thin near the tail and tapering thicker at the thorax.

Wrap hackle parachute-style around wing.

Whip finish, and cement the head. Sprinkle with garlic butter. A parsley garnish is optional.

In fly-tying, as in cooking, the results are only as good as the ingredients. To make good flies you must use the best possible materials. Spare no expense. Use only the finest hooks—high-carbon steel, chemically sharpened to a needle point, with subtle barbs that can easily be pinched. Use hackle so thin, long, and web free that you can tie two or three buoyant dry flies from a single feather. Deer hair should be luxuriously thick to keep bugs floating high. To make choice counterfeits, flies must be constructed with choice materials: It's a given.

A few accomplished fly tiers are so enamored of the craft that they don't bother fishing, but most—like most cooks—follow their passion to its logical consequence. Every fly whip-finished and removed from the vise represents a possible encounter on the water. Each saucy nymph could be the one to fool a twenty-inch rainbow; each bold streamer could incite a striper to charge through the surf; each neatly trimmed deer-hair popper could be the one that is blasted by a six-pound largemouth in the lily pads.

One bonus of tying your own flies is that it helps buffer the downtime between seasons. Sitting at a tying desk on a winter evening—by general agreement the best time to be there—is a fine opportunity for indulging in unbridled reminiscence. Flies are such compact packages of color and texture that they make potent mnemonic devices. A finished fly displayed in the jaws of a vise can conjure up the hoisting bulge of a trout taking a dry fly. It can remind you of a steelhead surging forward, engulfing your fly, and turning downstream in one elegant and murderous motion. It can bring to mind a northern pike launching from a weed bed next to the boat with the devastating accuracy of an arrow fired from a bow.

One of the standard streamer patterns just about everyone ties is a Woolly Bugger. It's so simple and easy to make that there's no excuse not to have an abundant supply on hand. The tail is a clump of marabou feathers. The body is chenille, wound the full length with saddle hackle. For variety you can tie in a few strands of tinsel or Krystal Flash. There are variations, but that's basically it. Fish it slowly, near bottom if possible, and give it action to make the marabou move in interesting ways.

Although I've caught a lot of fish with Woolly Buggers, I use them less often than a modification called a Bow Bugger. A Bow Bugger is a Woolly Bugger with an attitude. The only difference is it is constructed with a bullet-shaped deerhair head, but the head makes all the difference. I'm told it was first tied for Alberta's Bow River, where it proved deadly on that fertile stream's overfed browns and rainbows. A regular Woolly Bugger is enticing, but a Bow Bugger is *meaty.* Tied on a big hook, it's a mouthful. Brown trout seem to consider it their duty to annihilate the thing.

It's a pattern I can't tie quickly, so when I tackle half a dozen in an evening I have plenty of time to think. I remember a peculiar incident one evening in early July on the Manistee, when Glenn Wolff and I waded upstream from Yellow Trees, hoping to find a Hex hatch. I was fishing a small rubber-legged caddis imitation of a type that is often productive on that river, but this one was unique, tied by a young man in East Lansing who had asked me to try it and let him know if it caught fish. It was a small elk-hair concoction with white rubber legs tied in an X so that they stuck out like the legs of a tick. I'd never seen a fly quite like it.

Not far above the first bend, an old spruce tree had fallen into the river and died. Its needles were gone, and its naked twigs and branches formed a brittle and impenetrable lid over the water at the outside of the bend. I cast the caddis imitation and let it drift downstream almost to the tree and pulled it away. The next cast I got sloppy and missed the spot I wanted by about eight feet horizontally and six feet vertically, wrapping the leader in one of the branches. The water was too deep to wade and the fly was too far off the water to reach anyway, so I broke off the rubber-legged caddis and tied on a different pattern and moved on.

We worked our way upstream a half mile or so. I caught nothing and Glenn caught a single small brook trout. The Hex spinners never appeared, so when it was fully dark I tied on my biggest black Bow Bugger and started fishing back the way we had come. A Bow Bugger is a good fly to use at night. It displaces a lot of water, so trout don't have trouble locating it in the dark. I cast automatically as you have to at night, each cast direct and short, as close to cover as I could get it, lengthening my line a little each cast until the fly slapped against the far bank. But then I cast too far and felt the line go over an obstruction. When I pulled back my fly was hung up in branches across the river. It was too dark to see what I was hooked to.

There's nothing subtle about night fishing. I was using ten-pound-test leader, so I pulled until limbs cracked. My line came back dragging a small branch. I lifted it from the water and felt the tangled leader and switched on my pocket light and found my big wet streamer wrapped around a twig the diameter of a pencil. Beside it, less than an inch away, was the little X-wing caddis imitation.

Some patterns are more satisfying to tie than others. I like parachutes, partly because I learned to appreciate them late, but mostly because they're simple and symmetrical and come out looking like something a trout would fall all over itself trying to eat. The primary difference between a parachute and a traditional tie is in the placement of the hackle. Traditional dry flies have the hackle wound around the shank of the hook so the fibers stand out at ninety degrees. Parachutes employ a hackle wound around the upright "post" of the wing, so that the fibers extend parallel to the shank. That placement allows the thorax to float in the surface film instead of being supported slightly above it. Besides being realistically positioned on the surface, parachutes are durable and float well and seem to fool trout with slightly more than average frequency.

I've had especially good luck with Kelly Galloup's Troutsman Brown Drake. It's made with a body of brown moose mane tied extended beyond the hook, with a few hairs left long and split apart to serve as tails. A clump of white calf's tail is tied upright for a wing (making the fly visible in low light), and reddish brown hackle is tied parachute-style around it. Whenever I tie the pattern, I remember a June dusk when a good hatch of drakes started coming off while Kelly, Pat Moore, and I were floating one of the local rivers after an afternoon passed banging streamers. Brown drakes overlap with Hexes on many Midwest rivers, so it's not unusual for large trout to take them as appetizers before the night's feast. We switched to our dry-fly rods when we saw the first drakes on the water shortly before dark. I was at the oars. We came around a bend and found a tree across the river, with the trunk a few inches under water. Pat, in the bow, said he thought we could get over it if we got a running start. I backed up, then rowed hard to build momentum. Just as the boat lurched over the tree trunk, Kelly shouted, "Look at that!" Directly in front of us, four feet away, was the swirling riseform of a large trout. A heartbeat later we went over it. Somehow we avoided clobbering the trout on the head.

Brown trout are among the jumpiest of wild creatures. They'll panic if they see you lift your hand thirty feet away. A single sloppy cast can send them into hiding for the day. So we didn't expect to see this one again. But when we turned in our seats and looked back, the trout immediately rose again. I hit the anchor rope and the boat jerked to a stop. Kelly stripped line and cast. He cast again, and the trout came to his fly and took it with confidence. It was a broad-flanked eighteen-inch male. A couple of bends later we spotted another player, a big fish taking duns with explosive rises. Pat was using the same parachute pattern as Kelly. He hooked the trout on his second cast, and it jumped as if it had been jabbed by a fork. It got off a second later. Pat and I couldn't see it clearly when it leaped, but Kelly said it was big. Scary big. The kind of trout that can haunt you all winter.

SMALL FLIES ARE often easier to make than larger ones, if only because it is not quite so critical that you get every detail right. Trout can be infuriatingly selective during hatches of very small insects—I'm thinking particularly of the *Trico* hatch—but it is often only necessary to get the size, general shape, and approximate color correct. The smaller sizes of blue-winged olives—a generic term for the dozens of *Baetis* and other mayflies that hatch everywhere in North America—can be tied relatively quickly. I try to keep a small box stocked with a variety of them, including no-hackle patterns, comparaduns, and parachutes, but I lose tiny flies by the gross and can never seem to keep up. Blue-winged olives often attract only small trout, but you never know. Sometimes the big boys come to eat.

I remember years ago canoeing a river in the western Upper Peninsula, drifting beneath massive white pines at the foot of the Porcupine Mountains. In a broad pool at the outside of a bend, a very large trout swirled on the surface maybe fifteen feet from me. The swirl was bathtub-size, and the spotted tail that lifted above it was the width of my canoe paddle. There was no time to fish that day, but I made plans to return.

I had my chance midmorning on a cloudless day a year later. Hiking the shore, I was unable to find the same sweeping bend, so I settled for a stretch of deep pools and riffles between waterfalls a half mile above Lake Superior. A trail worn smooth by hikers follows the river on both sides there. By picking my way carefully, I descended a steep bank to a patio-size platform of rock at the edge of the river, only a short cast from the base of the falls.

Circling slowly in the pool was a raft of white foam churned up by the falling water. Trapped in it, like pepper in meringue, were hundreds of blue-winged olives. Trout were feeding in the foam, their swirls creating momentary holes in it. I cast a tiny imitation into the stuff, and it promptly disappeared. A trout swirled. I raised my rod and felt the solid, throbbing weight of a good fish. It rolled on the surface, a rainbow of at least eighteen inches, then bolted downstream, whipping my loose line through the guides. There was no stopping it. In a five-second galloping rush the trout reached the fast water at the end of the pool and my leader, 6X to match the small fly, broke.

More trout rose now, some feeding so vigorously that tufts of foam were thrown into the air and scattered by the wind like dandelion fluff. The fish were big. I was a featherweight in a heavyweight bout, but I kept fishing until I had hooked and lost a dozen of the best trout of the season and was out of blue-winged olives.

I think of those trout often. Every summer I'm sure I'll make it back to the falls during the hatch and try again, and every summer something comes up to keep me from going. But if the chance arrives, I'm determined to be ready. This winter I'm going to fill an entire box with nothing but blue-winged olives. It's a small plastic box, nothing special, but I like the way the little flies line up in it. It contains only a dozen or so now, but I'm certain that by spring it'll be overflowing.

An Apology for Ice Fishing

On very cold days, when your fingers ache and your ears burn and the wind brings snow in a continuous blinding drift across the lake, it's easy to agree with novelist and sportsman Jim Harrison: Ice fishing is a moronic sport. But only on very cold days. Much of the rest of the time it can be downright idyllic, not to mention productive, not to mention fun. Because ice fishing depends on so little equipment, chiefly a line and a hook, it is one of the most elemental ways to fish. The equivalent form of hunting might be snaring snowshoe hares with piano wire.

I came to ice fishing at a young age, and in desperation. The months from December through March were too long to tolerate without some kind of fishing, and in northern Michigan most of the kinds available happened to be through the ice. When I was presented with a new fly rod for Christmas one year, I rigged it with a wet fly and spent the afternoon standing on the ice casting into a narrow strip of open water in the channel between Long and Mickey Lakes. The water was about two feet deep, the bottom clean sand, and of course I caught nothing. I gave up finally and went home, where my father and I baited tip-ups with minnows and hauled in enough walleyes for dinner. The fly rod stayed in my closet until spring.

Ice fishing has not inspired a great deal of celebratory literature, largely, I suspect, because it is simple to learn and requires no fancy gear. Nor is it a sport that invites ponderous reflection. Cold weather itself seems to be a limiting factor, reducing thoughts to a small dull bundle of immediate impressions. But in discerning moods I am struck by the contrast between the flat and apparently sterile surface of the frozen lake and the life hidden beneath it. On the lake you are standing on the roof of a rich, vital, and diverse world filled with algae, zooplankton, insects, crustaceans, shiners, perch, and walleye, all of them part of a complex web of energy exchange that begins with sunlight filtering through the ice and ends with a pike pulled kicking from the water. Hooking a fish through the ice confirms that life flourishes in even the most inhospitable corners of our planet.

In my family it is traditional on Christmas Day to set tip-ups on the lake in front of my parents' house. Some years it is just my father and I who fish; other years my mother, my brother and sister, their spouses, and my wife and sons all get involved. We place our lines in a loose semicircle just beyond the drop-off, build a fire on the ice near shore, and stand around talking and waiting for the tip-ups to pop. If the ice is good, we shovel a rink and skate while we wait. Always, no matter what we are doing, everyone keeps an eye on the tip-ups.

A tip-up baited and set is a pure embodiment of potential energy. At any moment that latent loop of taut possibility can become unleashed, leaping upright, its small square of red cloth waving back and forth as if crying, "Me, me, attend to me!" Stare long enough at tip-ups on a frozen lake and they seem to tremble with the urge to be set loose. They are so potent that they often make regular appearances in my dreams. I see a flag upright above the snow and know that a fish has taken the bait and is running all the line off the spool. I am excited, but when I try to run to it I discover that I'm stuck in snow so deep I can't move.

Our Christmas outings have always been unpredictable. Some years we catch nothing, others we catch fish steadily through the day and into the night. We went all day a few years ago without a flag, and by evening, with darkness creeping over the horizon, I tended the lines alone while everyone else was up at the house getting ready for dinner. When it was nearly dark, my father came out on the porch and called for me to come up to eat. I started for shore but had gone only a few steps when a flag went up with a metallic click. I walked toward it and another flag popped, then another. In ten minutes I landed four walleye weighing from three to five pounds each. They lay on the ice tangled in line while I struggled with useless fingers to sort them out and rebait. Dad stepped onto the porch again.

"You coming up?" he shouted.

"I'm *trying* to!"

When I was sixteen we discovered brown trout in Long Lake and ice fishing took on a new seriousness for me. Until that winter nobody believed there were trout in the lake, though it was not a surprise to me. During the previous summer I had walked a stretch of shoreline one morning casting for smallmouth bass and had seen a brown trout perhaps fourteen inches long swimming in the shallows. It was a streamlined and graceful fish, its orange spots haloed and set in cream, but it was not healthy. A patch of fungus grew on its flank, and when it swam it faltered and veered, barely able to keep upright.

But why was it there? Long Lake is located in a region crossed by many rivers and creeks that hold browns, brookies, and rainbows, but the lake itself has always been a warm-water fishery. It was home to pike, walleye, smallmouth bass, and panfish. I had never heard of anyone catching a trout from it.

Yet here, unmistakably, was a brown trout, and one feeble enough, I hoped, to be careless. I held my breath and cast my nightcrawler. But the bait and sinker splashed too loudly, too close, and the trout darted away toward deep water and disappeared.

My friends didn't believe me when I told them what I had seen. They insisted that there were no trout in Long Lake. Even my father doubted it. If it was a trout it was a stray, he said, a refugee from a tributary stream. Soon I had doubts myself. By winter I was ready to believe I had been mistaken.

That year the ice was not strong enough to be walked on until the day after Christmas. We were on it before daylight. My father, my brother, our neighbor Dave Hardy, his son Brad, and I set a long row of tip-ups over a submerged ridge beside the island. We had fished that ridge many times and knew its subtle rifts and slopes, even beneath the ice and twenty feet of water. We sensed whether our bait was suspended over an unproductive flat or in the better water three feet deeper. It was a good place for walleye, but we also caught occasional pike and even smallmouth bass there. We were never certain what we had hooked until we fought it close enough to see it through the hole.

Lakes in northern Michigan rarely freeze clean. Most winters the first freeze comes during heavy snow, causing the ice to turn milky and weak and become layered with so much slush it is unsafe even when six or eight inches deep. But that was a rare year. The nights for the past week had been very cold, and there had been no snow or wind. The ice was as hard and clear as plate glass. Near shore we could see through it to the bottom, could see colored pebbles and birch leaves and the riblike ripples left in the sand by autumn waves. Farther out the bottom dropped away dramatically and revealed spooky blackness. The ice was three inches thick, plenty strong enough to support us, but it required courage to take those first tentative steps over the deep water.

It was brutally cold, and by daylight our fingers were numb from grabbing minnows in the bait buckets. We stood in a loose group near the island, stamping our feet and blowing into our mittens, all of us eager for the first flag of the season.

Over the years we have had many good days on the ice, days when school after school of walleye passed through, tripping flags as they went, days when the pike were so ravenous that they yanked the line from our hands before we could set the flags on our tip-ups. But we never had a day like that. The first flag went up shortly after the sun rose above the trees. As we started toward it, the one beside it popped. Then the next in line. Then the next and the next. Of the ten tip-ups we had set along the ridge, seven tripped in sequence during that first rush of activity.

We split up and went to our own lines. I leaned down and looked into the hole and watched my spool turning steadily, evidence that a fish had the bait and was running with confidence. I waited until the spool stopped and imagined the fish turning the minnow in its mouth to swallow it. When the spool began moving again I lifted the tip-up, grasped the line, and set the hook with long hand-over-hand pulls.

The fish bucked against the pressure. It came fairly easily at first, then fought strong enough to take line. I gained it back and had the fish coming toward me when it veered toward the surface, rising the way a kite rises on the wind. I could feel a shudder as it struck the ice. It was trying to jump. I had never known a pike or walleye to do that, and I wondered if I had hooked a bass, though they were rare in winter. Suddenly the fish was running toward me so fast I could not keep up and it shot past just beneath the surface, as visible through the clear ice as if it were in an aquarium. It was a brown trout about eighteen inches long.

I fought it carefully then. When it tired and allowed itself to be led into the hole I grabbed it behind the head and threw it on the ice. I straightened up and shouted in triumph, but when I looked around everyone was hauling fish out of the water, and each was a gorgeous brown trout the size of mine.

The lake was not the same after that. Big pike, walleye, and bass had made the lake seem dark and mysterious, vaguely ominous, but with trout in it whole new possibilities opened up. There was glamour and promise, as if the bottom had been seeded with emeralds, rubies, and diamonds. The bright colors of the trout, their novelty and abundance, created a kind of enchantment. Here was a lake so bountiful it allowed us to haul jewels onto the ice.

We caught trout all winter. They traveled in schools and we either caught a limit of them or we caught none. They would show up for two or three days in succession, then they would disappear for a week. A few anglers at the other end of the lake discovered them also, but we were all careful to keep our mouths shut. None of us had a sure explanation of how the trout had gotten into the lake, but rumors flew. Somebody said he had seen a Department of Natural Resources hatchery truck parked beside the lake a couple of years earlier; someone else said he had heard that a truck filled with fingerlings slated for release in Grand Traverse Bay had to dump its cargo into Long Lake when the aerator broke in passage. It wasn't until the following winter that the word leaked and clusters of shanties showed up near the public-access sites. Even after that the fishing remained terrific. Every year we caught fewer trout, but they were two or three inches larger than the year before. Eventually they all measured more than two feet long. The last one I caught weighed nearly eight pounds.

It would be twenty years before I met Stan Lievense, the Department of Natural Resources biologist who had been responsible for planting the trout in Long Lake. When I asked him about it, he admitted that he intentionally kept the planting secret because he did not want the lake overrun with anglers. Besides, he was curious. He wanted to see what would happen.

On Christmas Day we still go to my parents' house and set tip-ups for walleye and pike. There are no trout in the lake now, and walleye have been planted year after year in such numbers that it is unusual to catch any over fifteen inches long. But we don't mind. Pike seem to be making a comeback, and the muskie that were planted a few years ago prowl the drop-offs getting fat on a diet of stunted walleye. When I walk out on that flat white surface and cut a hole in the ice, I feel the old enchantment. I lower a line into the water, and it's like groping blindly inside a cave you suspect hides precious gems. If you're persistent and lucky you can sometimes find a few.

A Good Winter Storm

ONCE WE WOULD HAVE BEEN ALERTED BY THE THROBBING of an arthritic knee or by the restless lowing of cows in the barn, but now the first warning of the storm comes from a fast-talking television meteorologist who can't hide his enthusiasm. Wisconsin is getting hit hard, he says, and we're next in line. He rubs his hands together in actual glee and rattles off a litany of meteorological catchphrases, explaining that winds with names like the Alberta Clipper, Saskatchewan Screamer, and Manitoba Mama are bearing down on us because a shift in the jet stream has forced frigid arctic air to curve south from Canada like a streamer of smoke behind a train.

If we poke our heads outdoors we notice signs: the way

the day is held in pincers by a calm that is not quite the calm before the storm, the sky low and shifting in general sluggishness like a bad mood, the air heavy, the mercury in the thermometer hovering a little below freezing and about to plunge. There's a sure sign as well down at Mapleton Market, where people are stocking up on bread, milk, microwave popcorn, and videocassettes and are so talkative and friendly they're on the brink of giddiness.

Something in us loves a good storm. It forces our attention outside, away from the pull of televisions and computer terminals, and makes us aware of the natural world again. We seem to be a little hungry for it. Sometimes, of course, we get more than we want, but a storm in moderation is a good thing. It allows us to arm wrestle briefly with nature, and reminds us that we're Milquetoasts compared to that muscular lady.

On the meteorologist's radar the storm looks like the shadow of a giant bird flapping across the screen. We're told it will gain velocity as it crosses Lake Michigan and will pick up additional moisture from the relatively warm water. By the time the storm reaches the western shore of Michigan, the clouds will be black with freight and driven by winds of forty miles per hour.

Late in the afternoon pellets of snow begin to fall. They are flung by gusts and strike our front windows with a sound like thrown rice. All the birds have disappeared from the feeders and are hunkering for cover inside junipers and arborvitae, their stomachs filled with all the sunflower and thistle seeds they can hold. If the storm is prolonged, some of the birds will never leave the shrubs. We will find their desiccated carcasses in the spring. They will weigh almost nothing.

We're as ready as we can be, snug inside our bunkered house. The cupboards and refrigerator are full, wood is piled beside the fireplace, candles and flashlights stand ready on the kitchen table. Gail has a fat novel to read, and I have trout flies to tie. The children wear sweaters over their pajamas and ask for the tenth time if we think school will be canceled tomorrow. Yes, we think so, but we say nothing because we want no arguments at bedtime. We want the kids asleep at the usual time so we can sit together next to the fireplace with the lights off. We want to listen to the wind shout and watch snowflakes the size of bottle caps streak across the windows.

We wake in the morning to an unrecognizable world. Our yard is filled with sculpted drifts, and the north side of every tree is plastered with white. We turn on the radio and learn that schools are closed (and the kids bound cheering through the house) but that the storm has fallen short of the intensity and fury that makes a storm a blizzard—that apt word borrowed from early German settlers on the Great Plains, who after their first winters came away hollow-eyed and muttering about the *blitzartig* (lightninglike) way the wind and snow struck their homesteads. Our storm brings more holiday than hardship. When the sun appears I dress in heavy clothes, clear our driveway with the snowblower, and join the kids in digging tunnels through the drifts. By noon plows have cleared the road.

Storms of this magnitude occur half a dozen times each winter here in northern Michigan. A few a year might be considered blizzards (meteorologists define them as storms that have low temperatures, driving snow, and gale-force winds, thirty-nine to forty-six miles per hour), and one or two are real beasts. Once every decade or so comes a blizzard so notable it serves, like a death in the family or a move to a new house, as a milestone in our lives.

None of the storms of my experience can match the one my wife and I witnessed in 1977 when we were students at Northern Michigan University in Marquette, in Michigan's Upper Peninsula. Marquette is a compact city, built on hills that drop abruptly to the shore of Lake Superior, and is famous for the eighteen or twenty feet of snow it receives each winter.

When the wind is up and from the north it charges from Ontario across 150 miles of open lake, throwing enormous plumes of spray hundreds of feet inland and laminating every surface with ice. It is a place shaped and colored by weather.

Gail and I drove into Marquette for the first time on a bright January day when fog had slipped in from Lake Superior and left everything it touched covered with a furry coat of rime. Snow stood so deep that telephone lines were within reach of pedestrians on paths above the streets. We rented an apartment a few blocks from downtown in an aging house we shared with three housemates—all young men, a student and two lapsed students—who quickly became friends and shared meals, music, books, and our enthusiasm for the outdoors. The Boys, as Gail called them, were veterans of several Marquette winters. "Wait until it storms," they said. "You've never seen a blizzard until you've seen a Lake Superior blizzard."

One morning we woke to find the temperature outside had reached minus thirty-five degrees Fahrenheit. A few miles inland it was fifty below. When I stepped outside, I saw people up and down the street trying without success to start their cars, their hoods in the air like arms thrown up in surrender. My ten-year-old van started without difficulty, and I passed a neighborly hour giving jump starts. In the few minutes it took to step outside and attach the jumper cables to a battery, my ears, fingers, and toes would go numb and my nostrils would swell with what felt like walnut-size cotton bolls. Most of the neighbors were students from southern Michigan, who had never experienced such cold. We exchanged wondering comments, watching as the breath that hung around our heads crystallized and fell to the ground as fine snow.

The storm came a few weeks later. Clouds moved in that morning and the temperature climbed to the upper twenties, warmer than it had been in a month. The streets were coated with ice formed by snow that had been packed by traffic and frozen hard as concrete. All day the light was soft and strange, like the gloaming of twilight. On television the weatherman grinned and said, "Get ready, folks. It looks like we're in for a blinger."

It was cause, of course, for a party. We telephoned friends and told them to bring food, drinks, and sleeping bags, then laced on our ice skates and sashayed down the middle of the street to the Red Owl supermarket, where we were met at the door by a weary manager who put up his hands and said, "Hey, hey, this ain't Skate World." Inside we slid around the aisles in our stocking feet, loading a grocery cart with beer, chips, and frozen dinners, greeting everyone we met. Young people were animated and talkative, their eyes bright. Older folks acted the way they always acted.

We had noticed already that the people who boasted loudest about the difficulties of winters in the Upper Peninsula were usually recent immigrants, many of them from Detroit, a 450-mile drive south of Marquette, where winters are cold and damp but often free of measurable snowfall. Natives of the U.P., many of them descended from Finns, Swedes, and Italians who moved to the region in the nineteenth century to work in the iron and copper mines, were apparently too acclimated to the weather to give it much thought. To them win ter was not a romantic adventure or a Currier & Ives abstraction, but a fact of life, like unemployment, taxes, and backaches. Their stoicism could be extreme. Our second year in Marquette I worked for six weeks repairing railroad tracks on the Chicago-Northwestern line near Ishpeming, a town fifteen miles inland from Marquette. The crew of three included two native Yoopers (U.P.-ers), career railroaders who dreamed of being promoted to brakemen so they could spend their days riding in a heated caboose. I was taking a semester off from college to raise money and was grateful for the job, but I have never been so uncomfortable. It was a frigid, snowy November and the wind was relentless. In the cold the steel tracks cracked under the pressure of cars loaded with iron-ore pellets.

Our job was to cut out the broken sections and replace them with lengths of new rail. We did this by hand, unbolting existing track with four-foot-long wrenches, cutting broken sections away with a gasoline-powered hacksaw, driving new spikes with sledgehammers. One day when the wind was particularly agonizing and a harsh sleet lashed at our faces, I groaned and muttered something like, "Man, this is miserable." I sensed immediate disapproval from the others. Nothing was said but it was clear that I had violated a code.

That first winter no such codes applied, and we allowed ourselves to be awed by the weather. Outside the supermarket it had begun snowing—hard pellets that sheered at angles when the wind gusted, then dropped straight down and bounced along the street like excited molecules. By the time we got home from the supermarket, the wind blew with so much force that our house swayed, causing the water in the toilet bowl to rise and fall. The plastic sheeting our landlord had nailed over the windows bucked and snapped.

We turned up the music, made dinner, drank beer, laughed, and danced. Our friends arrived, loaded with supplies and talking in disbelief about the rising storm. Everyone took turns going to the door to watch the city get erased by whiteness. Gusts lifted snow into marauding clouds that swirled down the street and eddied into the openings between the houses, building drifts that by morning would reach to the eaves. Then stronger winds funneled in from the lake, carrying snow in streamers so thick we could not see the houses across the street.

A friend came late, red-faced and huffing, stomping his feet on the floor. He had abandoned his car in a drift blocks away. No way, he said, is anybody going anywhere tonight. Sleeping bags were spread, couches made into beds. We switched off the lights, and the wind came up louder than ever. It seemed to hoot at the pleasure of meeting obstacles.

In the morning all our windows were covered with elaborate, finely patterned frost that fell in curls to the carpet when we scraped it with our fingernails. We breathed on the glass until face-size holes opened and we could look outside. The wind continued to blow, sweeping loose snow down the street. Trees looked shocked and naked. Even the telephone poles seemed bent in misery. Our neighbors' houses appeared deserted, their driveways filled with drifts that covered cars to their roofs. Someone turned on the radio, and an announcer said in a cheerful voice that the state police had blocked all highways out of the city and classes at the university were canceled.

It was perfect. It was why we had come to Marquette: to be tested by extremes of nature, to watch the world throw tantrums. Staying warm in the midst of all that cold and wind made us feel capable and self-reliant and mildly heroic. We turned up the music and danced around the living room cheering for ourselves.

We were brewing coffee and scrambling eggs when someone walked onto our porch and knocked. We opened the inner door, then pushed hard on the storm door to break through the drift that had built in front of it. A swirl of snow and cold came inside.

Standing before us were two middle-aged women in bulky, snow-covered coats, headscarves knotted tightly beneath their chins. They looked like Russian peasants dressed to go to the market. Behind them snow roared down the street like invading panzers. The ladies smiled shyly. "We're collecting for da United Way," one said in the lilting Finnish accent of a native.

My friends and I were flabbergasted. "Did you *walk* here?" we asked.

"Ya. Down da street. It's our day for collecting."

It was unthinkable to turn them away. We invited them inside and filled their donation envelopes with our pocket change. We offered them breakfast, but they couldn't stay. They had many houses to visit, they said, and because of the condition of the streets they would have to do all their visiting on foot. They wanted to be finished in time to have supper ready when their husbands came home from work.

Big Trout in Condor Country

THE RIO PUELO IS BLUE. IT IS THE BOLD AND INAPPROPRIATE blue of a river in a child's crayon drawing. It is the blue of lapis lazuli, copper sulfate, and precious stones buried so deep they will never be uncovered. It is the color, you can imagine, of after-dinner cocktails on Jupiter.

I was in southern Chile, standing on the shore of this extremely blue river, when my guide, Arturo Redlich, said, "Good spot. Not long ago two fishermen here fish six, seven hours and catch sixty rainbows. Big rainbows, twenty-four, twenty-five, twenty-six inches. Is very good spot."

Arturo is the master guide of the river, the *jefe,* a fifty-something native of the city of Puerto Montt who has fished the region's trout waters all his life and spends his winters tying the flies his clients will use the following season. He takes the sport seriously. When he offered me one of his Woolly Buggers, I knew it was more than a casual suggestion. It was green with black marabou and tied with strands of flashy Mylar that in the water caught the light and made the fly shimmer like a bioluminescent creature at the bottom of the ocean. Here, near the river's end, a mile above the Pacific and still influenced by tide, the Rio Puelo is wide, deep, and powerful. A few days later we would watch a sea lion cavorting here with all the misplaced grace of a hippopotamus in a swimming pool.

I waded to where a band of clear water lined the shore. The clear water came from the Little Rio Puelo, a tributary that blends its crystal water with the big river's blue obscurity. Cobblestones of a dozen colors glittered on the bottom. I stripped line from my reel, false-cast, pulled more line, and cast the streamer far out into the Puelo. A short leader and a fast-sinking line carried the fly down quickly into the blue depths of the river. I mended the line to avoid drag and let the fly sink even deeper. When the line tightened, I began a pulsing retrieve.

A trout struck at the precise moment that the Woolly Bugger swam from the blue water into the clear. For a moment I thought it was another of the fifteen- and sixteen-inch rainbows we had caught all morning upstream. But this time, instead of leaping instantly from the river, the fish hung strong in the current, and I had the rare experience of leaning back on an eight-weight rod and being unable to move the fish. The leader was stout—the trout of the Rio Puelo are not leader-shy—and I put a lot of pressure on it. Still the trout stayed where it was, and I wondered if the line had twisted around a snag. Then the trout ran strong for the center of the river, and line ratcheted from my reel. I glanced at Arturo. There was no smile of triumph. In six days I had been unable to coax a smile from him. "Good place," he said. "Big rainbows."

IT HAD BEEN a cold winter in northern Michigan, one of the coldest in anyone's memory, and when snow still stood on the ground in April I was desperate to head south. But I went so far south that I passed right over the heat of the tropics and ended up at a latitude that is the mirror image of my own. Instead of spring it was autumn, with the same hard, metallic light and cold temperatures I had left behind. Afternoons were mild, but every night the snow on the mountains crept down a few hundred feet.

Whenever I hear about a place with world-class fishing I get skeptical. I don't necessarily doubt the report, I just know that no matter where you go, fish are fish. I've been in remote Canada, on lakes where northern pike strike so freely and viciously you better think twice about dipping your fingers in the water, and have seen the fish suddenly and inexplicably go into a three-day sulk that convinces you the water is barren of life. Just because you travel a long distance to fish doesn't mean you'll find the fishing trip of a lifetime.

I went to Chile prepared to see fine country but not necessarily to catch big trout. Never mind that I had been told by globe-hopping anglers that the waters I would fish are among the best for trout they've ever seen; never mind that I would be ferried to remote and seldom-fished rivers by float plane and helicopter, and assisted by guides who had spent their lives exploring the region. Trout are the same everywhere, I reasoned. I'll get skunked.

And I was right. The first morning on the upper Rio Puelo I caught nothing. My guide that day was Ocho, an eager young man of twenty-four who grew up on a ranch in the Rio Puelo Valley. Ocho's full name is Juan Ricardo Mancilla

Gallardo, but he was the eighth son born to his family and the numeric nickname stuck. He was an accomplished fly caster and a thoughtful companion on the stream, and planned to study English with a vengeance that winter at a school in Puerto Montt. I'm sure by now he is able to explain exactly where to catch the big rainbows and browns of the Puelo, a message he was forced to convey to me with gestures and stray words of tentative English.

Ocho and I had an understanding. He spoke about thirty words of English, and I spoke about twenty words of Spanish. Much can be communicated in fifty words. When I asked a question in his language, he answered as best he could in mine, and we spent a few minutes correcting one another. In that way we doubled our respective vocabularies in the week we fished together. In addition I loaned him some valuable English expletives and he loaned me a few Spanish ones. He taught me to say that the wind is a bitch, and I taught him to say, "Damned tourist." We laughed every time he said it. Soon we were thinking of ourselves as ambassadors of popular culture.

The morning I got skunked we had been ferried twenty miles upvalley by helicopter and dropped off at a log cabin on the bank of the river. Our plan was to fish all day, spend the night in the cabin with another guide, Irvin, who lives there alone during the trout season, and fish again the following morning. The cabin is located on a section of the Rio Puelo inhabited primarily by rainbows and is a short distance downstream from a major tributary, the Rio Ventisquero, which has a good population of both rainbows and browns. We would fish both rivers.

The Puelo is a big river even forty miles above the ocean, and the only way to fish it effectively is to travel upstream and down in boats and get out to wade the pools between the rapids. We used fourteen-foot, flat-bottomed aluminum boats equipped with powerful jet-propelled outboards, rigs that draw so little water they can shoot over shallows and roar upstream through rapids wild enough to make your throat go dry. The guides operate the motors by standing in the stern and are skilled at choosing the easiest routes through even the toughest rapids. Still, it takes some getting used to. A gringo accustomed to portaging class-three rapids finds himself clinging tightly to the gunwales.

Ocho and I motored upstream to a narrow gorge where the water was pressed between cliffs into a pool so deep it appeared to vanish into subterranean grottos. The water there was the same strange blue as downstream, tainted by copper deposits high in the mountains, but so transparent that I could see pebbles on the bottom ten feet below. Ocho had fished the canyon two days earlier with great success. He explained in pantomime how trout had risen from the depths to intercept streamers. But now they were being difficult. I tried nymphs and even dry flies, but nothing worked. Arturo and Ocho had already made it clear that this late in the season we could not expect to do well with anything but streamers. There is good dry-fly fishing in January and early February—Arturo described copious caddis hatches and five-pound rainbows picking dragonflies off the surface in the eddies—but this late in the season the trout would find only baitfish to eat.

We motored downstream, Ocho beaching the boat at every likely pool. I waded the edges and threw Buggers, expecting a strike every cast. But I caught nothing. I apparently set an unofficial record on the Puelo for the most consecutive hours without catching a fish. Ocho was saddened and bewildered. Communicating with gestures and a few words, he suggested we go back to the cabin and prepare lunch and wait for our luck to change. But I was determined to fish through the doldrums. "Uno more pool," I said.

We beached the boat at a broad scree of gravel beside the mouth of the Rio Ventisquero and walked up the tributary past the first rapids to a long pool. Casting one of Arturo's Woolly Buggers, I immediately hooked a twelve-inch brown, the first trout of the day. A few casts later I was stripping the streamer rapidly just beneath the surface, when a much larger trout arched up, rolled, and engulfed the fly.

Excited, I yelled, *"Mucho grande!"* which translates to "many big." I meant to say, of course, *"Muy grande,"* or "very big." Ocho came to my side, glanced at the trout thrashing on the surface, and shook his head. "No," he said. *"Es un poco grande."* A little big, or a little bigger than average. It was a nineteen-inch brown, with the hooked nose of a street brawler, and weighed perhaps three and a half pounds. I tried to explain to Ocho that it was many big compared to the trout I'm accustomed to catching back home in Michigan, but I don't think he understood.

When the trout tired I led it into the shallows. Ocho cradled it in his hands, unhooked it carefully, and resuscitated it until it swam off strongly on its own. I was encouraged to see Chilean guides, in this land where trout are so abundant, release every fish with such care, even reverence. Abundance breeds waste, but not everywhere.

TO THE EUROPEANS who settled the rugged valleys of the southern Andes, it must have been unbearable to see the rivers in that unspoiled land devoid of trout. Unbearable because the rivers are almost unbearably beautiful: cold and vital, so clear you can mistake a pool six feet deep for an easily waded three-footer, so lively during their tumbling descent through the mountains that the water is supersaturated with oxygen and supports a varied and rich biomass, from microorganisms to aquatic insects to the protein-rich pancora crayfish. In the late nineteenth century, trout were planted in rivers across Argentina and in high mountain lakes that straddled the border with Chile. One of those lakes was Lago Puelo, the birthplace of the Rio Puelo, which exits the lake and cuts west through a deep valley across Chile to the Pacific. In time Argentine and European settlers migrated down that same valley, finding patches of fertile bottomland where they could graze cattle and sheep. The settlers brought more trout with them, browns and rainbows and brookies, and planted them in every river and lake they came across. A German settler with a private plane became a kind of Johnny Appleseed of trout shortly after World War II. He filled plastic bags with water and fingerlings and air-dropped them into the ponds scattered across the region. His bombing runs might explain why so many of the remote waters in the southern Andes are home to thriving populations of trout that have probably never seen an artificial fly.

Flying up the Rio Puelo Valley, you get the impression that you are traveling against the grain of time into a land overlooked by the twentieth century. About halfway up the valley, some twenty miles above the Pacific, is a broad natural lake, Lago Tagua Tagua. Both above and below the lake are many deep gorges, where rapids flow tight between sheer cliffs, but every mile or so is enough flatland for a tiny *campo* owned by people who spin their own wool, have no electricity, and may descend to the village of Puelo at the mouth of the river just twice a year—once in the spring to leave their children at the school in the village, then again in the fall to pick them up. The children attend school in the summer months because winter is too harsh for travel on the river, and there is no way to leave the valley except by river or by air. The neat ranches with their weather-silvered houses and outbuildings are hewn from the dense junglelike forests along the river and perched on steep foothills. Jagged peaks topped with snow tower above them, blocking the sun for all but a few hours at midday.

One day we flew over those peaks. We took off in a twin-engine float plane, a Grumman Aleutian Goose originally used for CIA surveillance in the Aleutian Islands, and flew upvalley above the winding river with the mountains rising on both sides above us. We left the main valley and banked into a pass and started climbing. We climbed over naked rock with permanent ice packed in the crevasses, into high terrain where the pilot told me he had recently landed in a helicopter and watched a pair of Andean condors soar overhead. One of the enormous birds—its wings spanned about eight feet—hovered barely fifteen feet above his head and watched him with a look that made him feel, he said, like prey.

We climbed until the pass we were climbing ended at a sheer wall and I was sure we would bank into another pass. But there were no other passes. We simply tilted up, accelerated, and climbed over a razor-tipped peak, snow poised for avalanche a hundred feet below our landing gear and rocks so close I could see the lichen growing on them. I'm not graceful in flight. My appreciation of the convenience of aircraft barely overcomes my conviction that there is something unnatural about leaving the earth. In Piers Paul Read's book *Alive* and the movie based on it, a commercial jet crashes and the survivors endure horrible hardships in the Andes, among peaks much like those we were skimming past. You can't fly over those jagged and utterly inhospitable mountains without imagining what it would be like to go down in them.

And then we *were* going down, banking into a quick descent toward a lake ringed by mountains and with a pair of tumbling rivers dumping into one end and a larger river emptying out of the other. We landed in the lake and taxied to shore, where a temporary camp of wall tents waited beneath the trees. "Brook trout," Arturo said, nodding in the direction of the lake. "Big brook trout."

SOME PLACES ARE better left unnamed. In a lifetime spent fishing for trout, I had never caught a brook trout more than sixteen inches long. But guided by Arturo, who rowed us in a Zodiac raft along the shore of the lake and downstream into the river, I caught and released six brookies, the first measuring sixteen inches long and each one after that bigger than the one before. And when the brook trout weren't hitting, the rainbows were. I lost count, but between us Arturo and I caught at least fifteen rainbows measuring eighteen to twenty-four inches long.

The best fish of the day was a twenty-two-inch, five-pound male brook trout as bulky as a steroid junkie and dressed in the garish reds and greens of spawning season. It came furiously to a green Woolly Bugger in the waist-deep flats just above the river's first set of rapids. We kept that one, ate him that night baked with red potatoes and washed down with a crisp white wine so good it made me want to stand on the table and sing arias. I felt just the slightest bit guilty—it would have been prudent to return such a fine trout to the gene pool—but I have done so little damage to the brook trout population of the world that it was easy to forgive myself. I have never eaten a more delicious meal.

Big trout are greedy. When they're in the mood, the rainbows of the Rio Puelo share with largemouth bass a tendency to be attracted rather than repelled by the splashing arrival of a fly—it means something edible has blundered into the water. Strikes are sometimes preceded by a finned wake charging across the river. I had almost forgotten what that looked like. It had been several years since I had seen a large trout chase a fly with its dorsal slicing the surface and a hump of water riding ahead of it like the bow wave of a submarine.

"Strike! Strike!" Arturo shouted, but the trout did the job for me, grabbing the fly and turning in the same instant, slamming hard against the line and dogging for bottom. Then it came to the top in a wallowing leap so clumsy I thought of a fifteen-year-old boy taking his first belly smacker from a diving board. The trout ran for the far side of the river, a hundred yards away, and my line went down into the backing before I could put on enough pressure to slow the run and bring the fish to the surface again. This time it came out of the water with more grace, and while it was in the air its colors—chrome washed with pink—seemed the perfect complement to the strange, otherworldly blue of the river.

Is it possible to be overwhelmed by colors? Maybe. I had spent all winter in a monochrome world where the only relief from the white of snow and the black of bare trees was the washed-out blue of an occasional clear sky. Here the river was one startling shade of blue, the sky another, and the mountains looming above us were green, brown, and gray, capped with brutal whiteness.

"Arturo!" I cried. "It's a rainbow! A big rainbow!"

"Many big!" he shouted, grinning like a schoolboy.

A Sport of Kings

NO RAIN HAD FALLEN FOR WEEKS THAT SUMMER IN Iceland, and the rivers were so low you could see salmon stacked below every rapids and falls. On the Nordura anglers using very small flies had raised a few fish, but they were skittish and the fishing was tough. Then, the day before I arrived, it rained: a steady, all-day shower that brought the river up a few inches (but did not muddy it; the Nordura never muddies), and suddenly everyone was catching salmon.

I was already stoked with enthusiasm as I bumped in my rental car up the rutted gravel road to the lodge above the Nordura. The outing had all the earmarks of a tease—I had just a day and a half to satisfy the craving of a lifetime. Since high school and maybe a little before, I had dreamed of fishing for Atlantic salmon. I blame Ernest Schweibert, whose evocative recollections of rivers past had stirred a passion for exotic places where big trout and bigger salmon could be enticed into striking artificial flies if they were presented with sufficient skill and a pure heart. Schweibert, the dean of the "Me and André" school of fishing writers, was just as eloquent about good wine, good food, and cultured conversation as he was about trout and salmon. When I read him I was a young fish-head with powerful longings and a lust for adventure but little appreciation for culture. The wine, food, and conversation didn't take, but the places did—and if you could believe the ravings of writers like Schweibert, one of the best places of all was Iceland.

The Nordura is considered among the top half dozen salmon rivers in the nation, but it is not the best. That didn't matter to me. In the last few days I had seen enough of Iceland to know that the river and the country it passes through would be spectacular. Much of the big uninhabited interior of the island is a volcanic wasteland strewn with charred rubble that makes it appear as arid and lifeless as the surface of Mars. Some of it softens into bleak rolling fields with the winter-scarred look of Montana in spring, but most of it is covered with such recent volcanic debris that not much lives there. In the interior every horizon is wedged between volcanoes, some of them clearly active. Along the coasts the land is rich with meadows of wildflowers and stands of prolific, stunted birches. Here and there the ground is so thin it shudders beneath your feet and radiates enough heat to melt the soles of your shoes. Springs of hot water support lush, steaming thickets of ferns. Rivers are everywhere—winding through jumbles of rock, slicing in torrents across the lava fields, twisting down tawny meadow valleys where sheep and ponies graze.

The rivers of Iceland are either glacier- or spring-fed. Those that originate as meltwater draining from the island's five major glaciers tend to be fast and brutally cold and contain so much pulverized rock that they are the color of milk and can't support fish. The rivers born from springs are also fast and cold, but their water is clear and home to resident brown trout and Arctic char. During the summer they fill with Atlantic salmon.

"You have chosen the best possible time to be here," the river warden said. His job is monitoring the salmon and making certain everyone who fishes for them has paid for the privilege. I stood behind my car in the parking lot, struggling into neoprene waders and fumbling with the laces of my wading boots. An Englishman loading suitcases and fishing gear into the car next to mine told me he had caught six immature salmon, or grilse, from a single pool that morning. "You will catch salmon this evening," he said with certainty.

I walked onto the deck of the lodge, a low, cedar-sided ranch located high above the river on top of a treeless bluff. Below were two miles of rapids and pools strung out along the valley. Even from that height I could see salmon jumping in distant pools. The river warden followed me onto the deck and watched the vaulting fish. "Truly," he said. "The perfect time."

Inside the lodge I was introduced to two Icelanders who had volunteered to be my unpaid guides on the river. Guides are not required in Iceland, but the nature of salmon fishing makes it a good idea to hire one. Salmon that have returned to the rivers where they were born tend to hold in only a few favored pools. An angler accustomed to fishing for trout can waste a lot of time casting into beautiful and beguiling water that never holds fish.

Magnus Sigurdsson was a forty-eight-year-old bookkeeper for a contractor at the NATO base outside Reykjavík. His brother-in-law, Kristinn Valdimarsson, was the manager and part owner of a printshop in the city. As we were introduced, the river keeper explained that Magnus and Kristinn had already fished the Nordura several times that summer and were now sharing the price of one rod. It meant that they would have to fish alternately, one casting while the other watched. I would share a beat with them.

We followed a steep, winding trail from the lodge down the side of the valley to Eyrin, one of the most productive pools on the river. During the long climb down, Magnus and Kristinn asked if I had ever fished for salmon. When they learned that this would be my first attempt, they were suddenly no longer content to merely lead me to good pools. They wanted to see me catch a salmon, even at the expense of their own success, and insisted I fish Eyrin from the south shore, where a long gravel bar allows an angler to cover all the best water. Upstream was an eight-foot waterfall with a fish ladder notched into the rock beside it. Water poured down the ladder like a plumbing disaster. The pool below the falls was long and deep and, Magnus and Kristinn insisted, full of salmon.

In Iceland the wind can be so continuous that it becomes less a phenomenon of weather than a feature of the landscape. That afternoon the wind was so strong that each time I tried to cast upstream into it the line was thrown back at me. The wind lifted spray from the waterfall and carried it downstream hundreds of feet. Waves on the river had their tops stripped off into horizontal banners. In the middle of that turbulence, at midstream, precisely in the spot I happened to be looking at, a large fish poked its snout out of the water. I muscled a roll-cast across the river and my fly, a small Jock Scott, was snatched by the wind and thrown down hard on the surface, landing by chance just upstream from where the fish had appeared. I yanked the line to take up slack and the fly skittered on the surface like a tiny, brightly dressed clown on water skis. A fish the size of an otter swirled behind it.

I roll-cast again, and again the wind grabbed the line and slapped the fly down at midriver. The line straightened, and the fly skimmed across the surface. It had traveled maybe six feet when a salmon came up and ate it.

I waited for an absurdly long time before raising my rod. I had been coached to do this. Everyone I talked to and every book I read said this was the only way to hook a salmon. If you tried to set the hook quickly, as you would with trout, you would pull the fly from the fish's mouth. Instead you must wait until the salmon turned and swam toward the bottom and tightened the line itself—only then should you draw up tight on the fish. I did as I was instructed, and when I finally lifted my rod I felt the throb of something heavy and alive. Then it was off.

I didn't know if I had waited too long or not long enough to set the hook. I had no idea. Across the river Magnus was shrugging at me and holding his palms upward. He called out but I could not hear his words in the wind. I calculated how many hours I had left to fish. Not many. It seemed likely that I had just blown my only chance at a salmon in Iceland.

THE ATLANTIC SALMON is supposed to be the anadromous equivalent of the muskie, the fish of a thousand casts. Though I would gladly have made many thousands of casts on the Nordura River, I had two problems. The first was time. My week in Iceland was filled with so many obligations and appointments it had been difficult to break free for even a day and a half of fishing. I was there on assignment, to write an environmental story for a nature magazine, and had already spent a day bobbing seasick in the Atlantic, been bussed halfway across the island on a tourist junket, and dined with and interviewed government officials, university professors, biologists, and fellow journalists. Only after jumping through a complex arrangement of bureaucratic hoops had I been given permission to fish for salmon.

The second problem was financial. Salmon fishing in Iceland, as in all of Europe, is distressingly expensive. My day and a half on the Nordura cost fifteen hundred dollars for fishing rights, plus three hundred for meals and a night at the lodge. The thousand-dollar-per-day fee for the right to fish goes to the property owners—the farmers who raise sheep in the fertile valley of the river—and it's firmly set. Not even residents get a discount. Some salmon rivers in Iceland are less expensive, but they are also less productive. A few of the best beats on the best rivers cost considerably more. I was lucky to find an opening on such short notice on the Nordura.

It's important to understand that this is not my usual gig. In fishing, as in other passions, I've never had to pay for it. I didn't have to pay now, either—at the last minute the tab was picked up by the Iceland Tourist Board—but the principle rankled. I've always felt strongly that rivers, lakes, and oceans belong equally to everyone, and everyone should have the right to enjoy them. I don't mind paying a reasonable fee for a license, knowing that the money goes to enforce game laws and otherwise conserve the resource. But a grand a day? Seven grand a week? Ten grand for a week with lodging? It goes against my egalitarian grain. If the Nordura flowed through northern Michigan and were owned by a consortium of landowners who were growing rich collecting thousands of dollars a day from jet-set anglers, I'd be the poachingest son of a bitch you ever saw. I'd sneak into the river at midnight, wearing camo and blackened face, and catch as many fish as I could. I'd be the Robin Hood of salmon, the most feared catch-and-release criminal in the land.

To a certain extent, of course, you always have to pay to play. Either you pay in effort—as in canoeing and portaging one hundred miles of wilderness river in Quebec to reach a pool filled with five-pound brook trout—or you pay in dollars. The payoff is a richness of experience, a stock of memories, stories to tell your grandchildren.

But when richness of experience is confused with being flat-out rich, somebody loses out. In Iceland the high cost of fishing for salmon excludes many of the natives from the sport. At a fly shop in Reykjavík I spoke at length with a bright-eyed grilse of a clerk who graciously answered my questions about salmon and took the trouble to select a dozen local fly patterns (at five bucks each) that he said were necessary for the Nordura. As it turned out, he could hardly wait to get through those preliminaries so he could pump me for information about salmon and steelhead in British Columbia and Alaska. He could not afford to fish for salmon in his own country and was obsessed with the fact that in the United States and Canada he would be allowed to purchase a nonresident fishing license for less than a hundred dollars and fish anywhere he chose for a year. He could hardly imagine it. Talking about it made him downright goofy with excitement.

Yet, to my surprise, few of the other anglers I spoke with considered salmon fishing an indulgence of the wealthy alone. Icelanders are fiercely proud that in their eleven-hundred-year history as a republic they have always rejected monarchy. That explains in part, perhaps, why fly-fishing for salmon in Iceland is enjoyed by the middle class, while in Scotland, Ireland, and Norway it has traditionally been the sport of kings. Of the dozen guests staying at the Nordura Lodge, the only foreigners other than me were a stiff and unsmiling German financier who was a dead ringer for a Hollywood Gestapo officer, even down to the scar on his cheek, and a Danish businessman and his twelve-year-old son who, when I congratulated him on catching a ten-pound salmon, told me in flawless English and not a hint of snottiness that he had caught a twenty-four-pounder the previous week in Norway. The remaining guests were all residents of Reykjavík who every year squirrel enough money away to take a vacation at one or another of their nation's sixty salmon rivers. They did not consider the cost unreasonable. They argued, in fact, that it protected the fishery by making it too valuable to abuse.

Economists figure that an Atlantic salmon caught in a commercial net off the coast of Iceland is worth about eight dollars to the nation's economy, while one caught in a river with a fly rod is worth about eight hundred. In 1991 the government of Iceland placed restrictions on commercial fishing in offshore waters and issued an experimental ban on netting in the estuary where the Nordura and its several sister rivers enter the Atlantic. The following summer, salmon came to the Nordura in twice the numbers of the previous year. Since then their abundance and their average size have increased steadily. For decades nets in the estuary had been set with mesh sizes that captured most of the large salmon and allowed only small adults and grilse to pass through. Such plundering of the genetic stock helped make Iceland's salmon smaller than those in many countries. On the Nordura before the ban, few fish over ten pounds were caught. Now they are becoming common.

For someone who grew up practicing lowbrow versions of angling, the traditional implements and strict protocols of salmon fishing produce mixed feelings. But after seeing one phantom salmon rise to a fly skating across the surface, the idea of fishing with anything less refined than a fly rod seemed shameful. Netting one from a trawler would be obscene.

SALMON FISHING IN Iceland is allowed only during two daily sessions, from 7:00 A.M. to 1:00 P.M. and from 4:00 P.M. to 11:00 P.M. The first evening, after we left the river at curfew, Magnus assured me that I had done all I could to hook the salmon that rose to my Jock Scott. "Sometimes they are simply impossible," he said. "But tomorrow is a new day. Tomorrow you will have many opportunities to catch a salmon."

Before dinner there was some confusion when a non-English-speaking member of the wait staff tried to give me a bottle of chilled white wine. As I reached to accept it, thinking it was a gift, the Gestapo officer marched up, clicked his heels together, and took the bottle from the girl's hand. He said a few words to her in German, and she blushed and became flustered. He then gave me a cold look and went to his table with the wine. He did not offer me a glass.

Dinner was at midnight. We were served smoked pork chops awash in a mysterious but delicious sauce, small Icelandic potatoes, steamed cauliflower, and afterward a flaming dessert the chef delivered amid raucous applause. The dining room's single long table was filled with ruddy-faced men and women talking in several languages about the day's fishing. The German stood and announced that he had caught seven salmon from one pool that evening, all on tube flies. Polite congratulations were offered, but I noticed disapproval on several faces. Tube flies are made by tying furs and feathers to the outside of small lengths of plastic or metal tubing, which when pulled through the water leave trails of bubbles salmon are said to find irresistable. Later I would learn that tube flies are frowned upon by traditionalists. They're considered barely a step above live bait.

Then Magnus stood and told everyone that I had raised a fish on a Jock Scott. The news created a stir. It seems that the Jock Scott has a long and revered history on the Nordura but in recent decades has gone out of style. That I chose to fish with that particular pattern during my first evening on the river, and that it attracted the interest of a salmon, was seen as serendipitous. I was whacked heartily on the back by five or six people. The German whacked harder than anyone.

When I went to bed at 1:00 A.M., it was so light outside that I stood in the window of my room and watched ponies grazing on the slopes across the valley. I awoke three hours later, the sun already high and bright, and forced myself to stay in bed until six o'clock, when someone in the hallway tinkled a bell. I leaped up and dressed.

After breakfast we left the lodge and drove along a gravel road that placed us beside the river well before the seven o'clock starting time. We had drawn a good beat, one with more productive pools than we could possibly fish in a day. Magnus and Kristinn offered me the choice of fishing with them or spending a couple hours by myself on the same pool where the German had caught his seven salmon the day before. I decided to start the day alone.

They dropped me off beside a section of river that snaked in big gleaming curves across a hayfield, among rolled bales the size of Volkswagen Beetles. Beyond the valley was a row of dark volcanic cones. Except for the volcanoes, the valley and river could have been lifted from central Idaho.

"Walk across the field," Magnus said, "and fish down quickly past the first bend. The best water is at the base of the second bend. You will see three rocks rising above the water. Fish around the rocks. The salmon will be there."

I followed his instructions, beginning in the upper water where riffles dumped into deep pools tight against the bank. I saw no fish. Near the bottom of the second bend I came upon not three but five rocks rising above the surface of slow, chest-deep water. Thinking it odd that Magnus had not counted correctly, I fished every inch of the pool, changing flies a half dozen times, carefully covering all the water above, below, and around the rocks. When I caught nothing, I walked to the bottom of the pool, where the slow current spilled over gravel into a chute of fast water. A salmon broke the surface of the chute. I looked closely and there, again, the head of a fish came up. Then I noticed three rocks nearly submerged in the turbulence. I had been fishing around the wrong rocks.

I cast my fly, a size 6 Rusty Rat, across and down, letting the line quarter in the current and sweep into the fast water where the fish had shown. Something strong pulled at the fly. It seemed to pluck at it, as if someone had gripped the fly between a thumb and forefinger and pulled. The sensation was so unusual that I was not sure it was produced by a fish and hesitated to set the hook. I lifted my rod tentatively and it bent. A salmon of about six pounds leaped immediately from the river. It ran the length of the chute into the rapids below and leaped again. I followed downstream along a gravel bar. When I could lead the fish into the shallows, I tailed it and lifted it from the water.

It seemed astonishing that this lovely, wild, powerful fish had taken a fly so eagerly—that it had come to the surface in pursuit of a colorful scrap of feathers that resemble no living thing and was presented in a way that intentionally induced it to drag. Such drag would send a trout diving for cover. Now I understood why monarchs through the centuries have claimed the fish and the sport for their own. There is something undeniably regal about the fish, something profoundly dignified about the sport. I thought of the first time I tasted a really fine wine: Until then I could not imagine what the fuss was about.

The fuss that surrounds salmon fishing reaches its most distilled form in the flies. They are constructed according to very old, very complex, and very carefully prescribed arrangements of feathers, fur, tinsel, and silk. Their complexity was probably originally intended to keep the riffraff from producing them. The patterns were given names like Blue Charm, Lady Caroline, Black Fairy, and Silver Doctor, and made as colorful and intricate as hummingbirds. Nobody pretends that salmon will strike only traditional patterns or only those made with the feathers of a dozen exotic birds. In fact, in Iceland one of the most effective patterns, the Collie Dog, is a simple streamer tied with a silver tinsel body and a dark wing made from the hair of a sheepdog—and not just any sheepdog, but a particular dog owned by the Scottish fly tier who produces the pattern. The fly's future is certain: When the Scotsman's collie dies, so does the Collie Dog.

During the next hour every tenth cast or so I felt the deliberate, pulling strike of a salmon. All the fish were holding in the fast water around the rocks or just below them. I landed only the first six-pounder and hooked two about the same size and had them nearly to my feet when they pulled free. One or two others felt larger during their first run downstream but got off before I could see them. One strong fish ran down into the rapids and broke my six-pound tippet. I shortened the leader, as Magnus had suggested, until it tested about ten pounds.

There would be other salmon that day. Kristinn caught a nine-pounder first cast in an unnamed pool below a road bridge, then hooked and lost three others all from the same spot. Magnus would cast his big fifteen-foot Spey rod with both hands hour after hour, never raising a fish and never complaining or losing heart. Late in the afternoon, in a narrow, rock-strewn canyon and a pool known as Leggjabrjotur—"break a leg," for the boulders that make wading treacherous—we saw a salmon surface in a table-size slick surrounded by fast current on the other side of the river. To reach the fish I had to make a steeple-cast that threw my line high against the canyon wall behind me and sent it fifty feet across the river. In what was certainly more a matter of luck than skill, my fly landed in the center of the slick. The salmon came up immediately and took it.

I saw no evidence of a catch-and-release ethic in Iceland. The salmon are so abundant that a kind of innocence reigns. I'm told that any angler who catches a salmon implanted with a Floy tag—an electronic device that allows biologists to track migration—and records the tag number and the size and sex of the fish before releasing it is rewarded with a bottle of Bacardi rum, a real windfall in a country where spirits are highly appreciated and extremely expensive. But every Icelander I saw catch a salmon killed it. When I suggested releasing my second fish, Magnus and Kristinn were horrified. It was inconceivable. Salmon were there to be caught and eaten. Throwing them back would be wasteful.

So I killed both of my fish. It was easy to justify. If the Nordura were public water it would be a different matter, but with only a few dozen anglers killing a few fish each per year, there is little strain on the resource. A commercial trawler would take ten times that many in a single day. And it would have been rude for me to release a fish without offering it to my guides. They stood beside me grinning while I bowed to tradition and sliced the small, fatty, adipose fin from the back of my first salmon and swallowed it with a mouthful of river water. I gave the second fish to Magnus.

We had another late dinner and took silent pleasure when the German admitted that his tube flies had failed him that day. Magnus, Kristinn, and I toasted the river and the salmon. Magnus introduced me to his daughter, a radiant twenty-year-old law student who had come for the evening to visit her father. I told him she was beautiful, and his eyes filled instantly with tears.

I drove in twilight the two hours south to Reykjavík, slowing for sheep that had wandered onto the highway. As I crossed rivers rushing from the interior toward the coast, I thought of the Icelanders who fish for salmon in those waters—the shopkeepers, accountants, and high-school teachers who save their money all year for a week or two of fantastic fishing. They would deny that casting elaborate flies for salmon is a sport reserved for the privileged classes, would perhaps argue that in Iceland everyone is a person of privilege.

And what if those lively rivers were mine? What if I owned the land, the water, the salmon that swam up from the ocean to spawn? Would I gate the roads and post the boundaries and allow only my closest friends inside?

I stopped on a bridge over a river so lovely that I felt

something in my chest rip. Rapids tumbled toward the bridge, throwing whitewater hard against black volcanic rocks. Upstream, in pools so deep and clear that in sunlight the water would become as blue as glacial ice, salmon swam restlessly. For enigmatic reasons those fish would occasionally rise to the surface to take flies thrown by hopeful oafs who had traveled thousands of miles to sample the mystery and sustain the tradition. Sometimes tradition is just folly perpetuated. But not here, not now. And if it was, it didn't matter. I wanted more. I wanted much more.

Heaven help us if I ever strike it rich.

Fisherman's Weather

If there is virtue in humility, we anglers should be eligible for canonization. All those days beneath the sky, at the mercy of wind and storm, remind us that we are very small and very ignorant. Fishing and meteorology are among the most uncertain of sciences. Combine the two and you find yourself on shaky ground indeed.

Nevertheless, fishing and weather go together nicely, especially if you're the kind of fisherman, as I am, who spends less time catching fish than watching what's going on around him. What's going on, every moment, is weather. Since there is an indisputable connection between what the weather is doing and what the fish are doing, we can be forgiven for studying the sky with the aim of increasing our angling success. Some of us become soothsayers and shamans of weather lore, watching for telltale signs, reading auguries in weather forecasts, hunkering over our barometers like Gypsies over crystal balls. In the end we might not know why we're successful some days and unsuccessful others, but we can tell you the difference between cirrus and stratus clouds and anticipate with fair certainty if it will rain in the afternoon. We'll claim that when the wind is from the east the fish bite the least, and we might even believe it, though we'll probably go fishing in an east wind anyway.

I've been trying all my life to figure out the connection between fishing and weather, and finally must admit to being stumped. Most of my fishing lately has been on rivers for trout. Perhaps because they live in perilous places and often feed near the surface, trout are particularly sensitive to weather. They are often most active on days that are overcast, windless, and humid, and they can become frenetic eating machines during the glowering, static, expectant hours preceding rain. Under a gray, uniform sky they often venture into the open. When the day is sunny, they tend to seek cover in deep holes and beneath shore banks and logjams. Worst yet are bright days punctuated with drifting clouds. The shadow of a cloud passes over the water with the ominous foreboding of a bird of prey, and trout dash for cover.

But the rules are not set in stone. Most of the biggest brown trout I've seen caught from rivers in recent memory were taken with streamers around noon on sunny days. The rules also change with region and species. Muskie anglers, for instance, prefer bright, windy days over clouded, still ones. A few years ago a computer analysis of 550 muskie catches indicated that the most productive times to fish for those toothsome giants was on cloudless days with brisk wind blowing from the south or west. The least productive times were when there was no wind, when it was storming, and when the wind was from the north or east.

Much has been written about the abilities of fish and other wildlife to detect coming changes in weather. According to one theory the sensitive lateral lines along a fish's flanks can detect the rumbling of thunder when it is still too distant to be perceived by human ears. Another theory suggests that fluctuations in barometric pressure cause a fish's swim bladder to expand or contract, motivating it to move to deeper or shallower water to relieve pressure and reach ideal buoyancy. Another proposes that barometric changes alter the amount of oxygen at different depths, causing fish to rise or descend and thereby influencing their feeding behavior.

As far as I've been able to determine, none of those theories holds up to scientific scrutiny. The problem is a lack of hard data. Fisheries biologists are extraordinarily cautious on the subject. When I called a noted ichthyologist at the American Museum of Natural History, he declined to offer his opinion. Too many unknowns, he said. A biologist at a prominent university would say only that he doubted that anyone could answer my questions. He admitted that the weather almost certainly had a major influence on the behavior of fish, but not enough data were available to draw conclusions or venture opinions.

Anglers, as a group, are less stingy with their opinions. Bring up the subject and you're guaranteed to hear no end of observations, opinions, and prejudices. One guy will tell you that a sudden change in weather sends fish to the bottom in a petulant sulk and that you might as well go home and sharpen hooks until conditions settle down. Another insists that after a week or two of stable weather, a cold front or a change in wind will stir fish to fresh activity.

Ask if an approaching storm causes fish to feed, and you're almost certain to start a debate. An old proverb voices a popular opinion: "When trout refuse bait or fly, there is a storm nigh." An opposite stance is expressed by "Near the surface, quick to bite / Catch your fish when rain's in sight." The most often repeated ditty is probably: "Fish bite the least / When wind's in the east" (or a dozen variations, including my father's "Wind from the east / Goddamn fish go south").

Anglers with a prejudice against east winds note that in North America an easterly wind often precedes the counterclockwise rotation of a low-pressure center. For one reason or another, low pressure often means death to fishing. Yet, this past June I was with a party of four anglers who in three hours caught fifteen big trout and salmon from Lake Michigan while the wind blew straight from the east. And I've been skunked so many times during wind from the west, when fishing is supposed to be best, that I've learned a healthy skepticism about weather ditties of all kinds. Probably the best time to go fishing, as John Voelker said years ago, is whenever you can.

But many anglers—this one included—are convinced that when the fish are sulky, there's nothing like a good storm to turn them on. Kelly Galloup and two friends caught and released more than twenty steelhead one spring morning on the Pere Marquette just before a tornado ripped through the woods a hundred yards from them and filled the river with smashed kindling. They hooked steelhead as fast as they could cast and often had two or three on at once. The trout were so eager that they sometimes chased flies halfway across the river before striking.

Such behavior might have some logic behind it. Hard rain and wind knock insects off leaves, wash earthworms and other succulents from the ground, and deposit them in the water. Pavlov conditioned dogs to salivate at the sound of a bell. Maybe fish learn to salivate at the first grumble of thunder.

The relationship between bad weather and good fishing was made abundantly clear to me one day in Yellowstone National Park. That morning my wife and I had driven into the town of West Yellowstone to buy supplies and wash our clothes at a laundromat. In the afternoon, on the way back to our campground, we decided to stop off and fish a famous and popular section of the Madison River called the Barn Pools. Gail decided she would stay in the truck and read while I fished. The forecast was for thunderstorms, and she said she was anxious to get back to camp to put things away before the rain began. I promised to be quick.

I had grown up reading about places like the Barn Pools and regarded them as shrines that I must visit whenever I had the chance. But this particular shrine was disappointing. The parking lot was full of pickups and sport-utility vehicles, and anglers stood in groups talking and comparing gear. The river wound in a series of bends through a wide valley, and at each bend was a run of dark, promising water—the Barn Pools. The runs looked inviting but they were crowded. Three or four anglers fished in every pool and others were walking the worn trails between them. A short distance down the bank, two fishermen in cowboy hats took turns photographing each other in simulated angling poses. I asked how the fishing was and they made ugly faces and said it sucked.

But I was determined to sample all the famous water in the park, even if just to gauge it against the fabulous places I had already discovered. I had caught big trout from the Firehole and Yellowstone Rivers and from the very accessible Junction Pool where the Gibbon and Firehole come together to form the Madison. But none of those places had been as crowded as this. I decided to make a few casts, just to say I had fished there. My expectations were low. They were lower than low.

I was rigged up and wading into the shallows on the inside bend of the first pool before I noticed the sky. Clouds had been building all day above the mountains to the north, piling up like overyeasted dough in a baking pan. They had seemed harmless. Now they were dense and black and bearing down on the valley like masses of Attila's cavalry. The temperature was falling and the wind rising. Gusts flurried the water.

I tied on a large stonefly nymph and managed a sloppy cast into the wind that placed the fly midstream in the strong water at the head of the pool. Raindrops began falling with enough impact to raise spouts in the river. The wind took on a new and strident urgency.

When lightning flashed a mile down the valley, followed a two-count later by an explosion of thunder, people began running for the parking lot. They climbed into their cars and rolled up their windows. Many of them were parked close enough to watch me as I fished.

On my second cast a trout plucked the nymph almost the instant it hit the water, then jumped three or four times before I landed and released it. It was a rainbow about sixteen inches long. The next cast I caught a brown trout about seventeen inches long. Then I caught one about the same size. Then another, a little bigger. On each of the next two or three casts I felt the determined solid tug of a good-size trout but failed to hook it. I shot a low hard cast beneath the wind, and the nymph sank and something bigger than all the others took it with a furious slamming strike and plowed deep into the river, stripping line from my reel. I don't know how big it was. Very big. Bigger, perhaps, than any trout I had hooked that year. It stayed deep, out of sight, and pulled away with the power of a strong dog on a leash. I followed as well as I could along the bank.

By then the storm was directly overhead. The clouds rolled, convoluting dramatically as if captured by time-lapse photography. I was acutely aware that I was the tallest object in a valley where nothing stood higher than prairie grass. I knew I could die there. I thought of all the hapless anglers and golfers who had been struck dead in similar situations. Standing in the open during such a storm was a dimwitted thing to do, and I certainly don't recommend it.

But fishing like that doesn't come along every day. Not even every few years. I was on a famous river in magnificent country, hooked to what was likely the largest trout of the season, and even if I failed to land it I was positive I could catch others just as large. It was a form of madness, a greedy lust for success. For a few minutes I believed that death by lightning was a small price to pay to continue fishing.

The trout made a long run through the deepest part of the pool, then settled near bottom and shook its head back and forth. I had just begun to think it was tiring when it made a sudden brawling run downstream and broke my leader.

Lightning flashed overhead, followed so quickly by thunder that I wasn't sure I had heard anything at all until I realized my ears were ringing. It felt as if somebody had smacked the side of my head with a tennis racket.

Then the rain came. It did not fall, it plummeted. It came down with so much force that all the tall grasses were immediately flattened, making me an even more conspicuous target on the landscape.

I ran for the truck. As I sprinted past cars in the parking lot I could see people watching through the windshields, their faces showing expressions of what looked like admiration and envy.

Gail pushed open the door and I dived inside. "Did you see that?" I croaked. "That trout was *huge*!"

She looked at me intently for a long moment. Finally she said, "What you just did was so stupid that I can't talk right now. I don't want to hear a word about it. Just shut up and drive."

For years afterward I tried to get far enough ahead of thunderstorms to make a few casts. I caught fish, but never as many and never as large as those I caught that afternoon on the Madison. I still fish before a storm every chance I get, but I no longer think of it as a sure thing.

I'm convinced, in fact, that there are no sure things, not in fishing, poker, and romance, and I'm deeply suspicious of any theories that guarantee instant success of any kind. Most of our theories about fishing are little more than earnest silliness. They keep us occupied in the off-season but have very little practical use.

The truth is, nobody knows beans about what makes fish bite the lures we toss so optimistically into the water. I prefer it that way. Let the scientific anglers debate questions of technique and behavior until the cows come home. I'll be out on a river somewhere with a fly rod cradled in my arm, watching the water and the sky and trying not to miss anything. There's enough going on out there to keep a humble guy busy for a lifetime.

Last Day

MIKE MCCUMBY WORKS TOO MUCH. I KNOW HE'S A little tired of hearing it, but it's true. He's a building contractor who always takes the extra time to do a job right, even if it means working evenings and weekends. He and his wife, Marcy, and their two children live in a small town about a mile from one of Michigan's famous trout rivers, in an eighty-year-old farmhouse they've been remodeling for a decade or so. When Mike's not building other people's houses, he's replacing kitchen cabinets at home, cutting firewood, gardening, gathering apples from the trees in the yard, attending his children's basketball games and dance recitals, and assisting relatives and neighbors with their domestic emergencies. He also hunts deer and turkey and fishes for trout. Or he used to. Lately he's been too busy.

Mike and I have been fishing together since high school. For most of those years there have been three angling events we never missed, no matter how hectic our schedules: opening day, the Hex hatch in late June, and the final day of the season. But lately work and other obligations have kept Mike busy even on those sacred days and nights. He says if trout season were compressed into two weeks, like deer season, he would get out on the water more. Months ahead of time he would be preparing gear, planning strategies, mapping destinations, and when the season finally arrived he would fish every possible minute of those fourteen days. But with it spread over five months it's easy to take the season for granted, to miss a week or two, to postpone a weekend outing because there is always another weekend to come. It's like youth. You think it will never end, but it does. One day you wake up and it's October.

We share the same basic situations: young families, houses in perpetual need of repair, the dizzying responsibilities of adulthood. But I get out a lot—it's my job, after all—and by the end of September I'm content to see the season end. Mike, last year, was not. All spring and summer, whenever I called, he said, "Maybe next week." When the trees began to flare with color and it was obvious that time was running out, I got insistent. The last day was on a Friday, a pretty good day for working stiffs. But he couldn't make it. Too much to do, he said. Maybe Thursday.

Thursday morning I stood in Mike's kitchen drinking coffee while he squirmed and made excuses and complained that an expensive parquet floor had come in special order and needed to be laid that day because the owners had a party scheduled for Saturday night. Finally Marcy took charge. The party was a week from Saturday, she said. The weather was too warm to put up storm windows. The woodpile could wait. Go fishing.

Mike looked at me and grinned. "What are we waiting for?" he said.

AUTUMN IN NORTHERN Michigan hasn't peaked by the end of September. Tamaracks, which in a few weeks will yellow and drop their needles, are smoky with impending fade. Sugar maples, always the first to color, are scarlet or yellow or orange, but the leaves of oak, ash, and aspen remain mostly green. By the time the woods are in their full brilliance, trout season will be over.

While it lasts, that autumn fishing can be very good. The rivers are usually in good shape, the water clear, the bottom vivid with colored stones and fine, emerald algae. On the surface the water glints blue and gold and khaki, each riffle tipped with glittering bits of mirror. Trout rise to feed on terrestrials, *Baetis,* caddis, and other small autumn bugs.

Bird and deer seasons are just ahead, but if you want to fish—and I do, year round, even when snow covers the ground and the guides on my rod fill with ice—there is still much to do. Here in Michigan certain stretches of river are open until the end of December for steelhead and salmon, a few are open year round, and several choice lengths of blue-ribbon streams remain open for resident trout. You can fly-fish twelve months of the year if you choose.

But the rivers I like best are still subject to the traditional opening and closing dates. For seven months you can't fish them at all. I like it that way. It gives the trout a rest, permits them to spawn without being disturbed, and allows the imagination time to incubate. Like fields left fallow, those waters are better for being unfished most of the year. I think we benefit from such closure. Some things are worth waiting for, are better for having an opening and a closing and being sometimes unattainable. How magical would deer season seem if it lasted six months? How many duck hunters would be awake all night before the opener if the season began in August and ended in January?

MIKE AND I drove to the upper river. The water there is bright and quick, its riffles slowing in pools that flow dark green beneath the cedars. The river is inhabited by both brook and brown trout. Local bait fishermen catch hog-size browns there, but most of the flycasters I know take only occasional sixteen-inchers, except during the Hex hatch, when bigger fish are caught with some frequency. But you rarely see big fish feeding during bright September days. You learn to lower your expectations.

We bushwhacked through a quarter mile of hardwoods, then followed a game trail down a long, steep bank into the alder bottoms. The trail peters out there. You have to weave your way through as best you can, keeping your rod pointed ahead like a directional antenna. Mike and I once got lost in this same swamp at night after fishing the Hex hatch. We discovered after it was already dark that I had forgotten my flashlight and that the batteries in Mike's little vest light were so weak he could scarcely see to tie on a fly. At midnight, trying to find our way back to the car, we got turned around in the tag alders. It was a cloudy night and moonless, so there was no help from the sky, and it was too windy to hear the river. We were in no danger—the swamp is bordered by the river on one side and the gravel road on the other—but we managed to stay lost for an hour.

Now, in daylight, it took only a few minutes to push through those fifteen acres of alders. We broke out next to the river and found it covered with flying ants. That's not unusual in September, when ants abandon their nests, sprout wings, and fly off to establish new colonies. Thousands of them take to the air at once and blunder around clumsily. When they blunder onto the water they become easy food for trout.

The ants were tiny, reds and blacks about evenly mixed, their transparent wings gleaming in the sunlight. They drifted among a few early leaves, on water the same cold and metal-blue color as the sky, and were picked off steadily by small, eager trout in the shallows and by larger, more deliberate fish where the current was strong and deep.

We saw a good trout rise quietly against the far bank, where grass leaned over and dragged silently in the water. Mike tied on a cinnamon ant and waded into position below the riser. Aspens and cedars formed a canopy over him, and he had to cast sidearm to keep his fly out of the branches. His ant landed among drifting leaves, and when he lifted it to backcast, a yellow maple leaf came with it.

"Salad," he said. "Diet food." He gave the trout a few moments, until it fed again, then made another cast. The trout rose and he hooked it. It was a brookie, its colors as hard and bright as river pebbles. It might have stretched to nine inches.

A decent fish rose downstream, and I waded to within casting distance. I put on a black ant girdled with a few turns of hackle, dressed it with floatant, and cast over the fish. It took the fly without hesitation, and I drew up tight on a twelve-inch brown.

And so it went. Trout rose all afternoon. A few mayflies came off late in the day, and we switched from ants to blue-winged olives. It didn't seem to matter. The fish would take any carefully presented fly. Between us Mike and I caught and released a few dozen. We saw no other anglers, though at dusk a canoe came downstream carrying two deer hunters scouting locations for Saturday's bow opener. "When's this river close for fishing anyway?" one of the hunters asked. "Tomorrow," Mike said.

We left the river and pushed through the tag alders and

climbed the long hill to the truck, then drove to a tavern for burgers and beer. One beer led to another.

Finally there was no putting it off. We made promises to get out more often next year, to not let work get in the way of what was important. We shook hands and said our good-byes.

THAT SHOULD HAVE been the end of it, a satisfying conclusion to the season, a tidy wrapping up of the year. But Friday morning was warm and windless, fishing weather, and although I began the day with the best of intentions, I could not keep my mind on my work. I thought of how the first day and the last day of the season are more important than all the other days put together. The first day, in youthful April, is filled with excitement and anticipation, fat with potential, a day to spend in cheerful and naive optimism. The last day should be taken slowly, like a last meal, so you can absorb enough sights, sounds, and scents to last through the winter. It is a day to spend sitting in a warm spot on the bank thinking of the season that is ending and the seasons yet to come. I fought it until noon, then caved in.

I parked in the same spot, walked through the hardwoods, slipped down the high bank, busted through the alders, and came out on the edge of the river. I had it to myself. It was a Monet day, the river shimmering like a watercolor painting. Ants were falling again and trout were rising. I forgot all about Mike. I claimed the place as my own and took a proprietor's interest in the yellow leaves dropping from the birches, in the methodically feeding trout. I saw a good fish across the river.

"That's no twenty-four-incher," someone said behind me. I turned. It was Mike, leaning against a birch, grinning.

"I thought you couldn't make it today."

"I thought *you* couldn't make it."

"You could have called me, you son of a bitch."

"And *you* could have called *me*."

I offered him first chance at the fish across the river, but he took a seat on the bank. "I'd rather watch," he said.

We made our way upstream, taking turns on risers, the river wide enough to accommodate only one of us at a time. We caught fish, not so many as the day before, but enough to hold our interest. Time became irrelevant. The hours drifted away.

Late in the afternoon, with the sun almost gone, Mike tied on a small Royal Wulff and made a long cast that settled the gaudy fly among floating leaves. They drifted together, the colors of autumn surrounding the jewel-bright red of the dry fly. In the next half hour Mike hooked and released five brookies up to ten inches, then a brown a little over a foot long that took the fly with the authority of a much larger fish and burrowed deep into the current. Mike bent to the river and released the trout. He joined me on the bank, and we sat and watched the sun disappear behind the maples on the ridge above us.

Mike clipped the bright fly from his leader and stuck it in the bill of his hat. It was the final moment of the final day of the twenty-fifth year we had been fishing together. Then the moment passed and it was time to go home.

Stories

The Pond at Millbrook

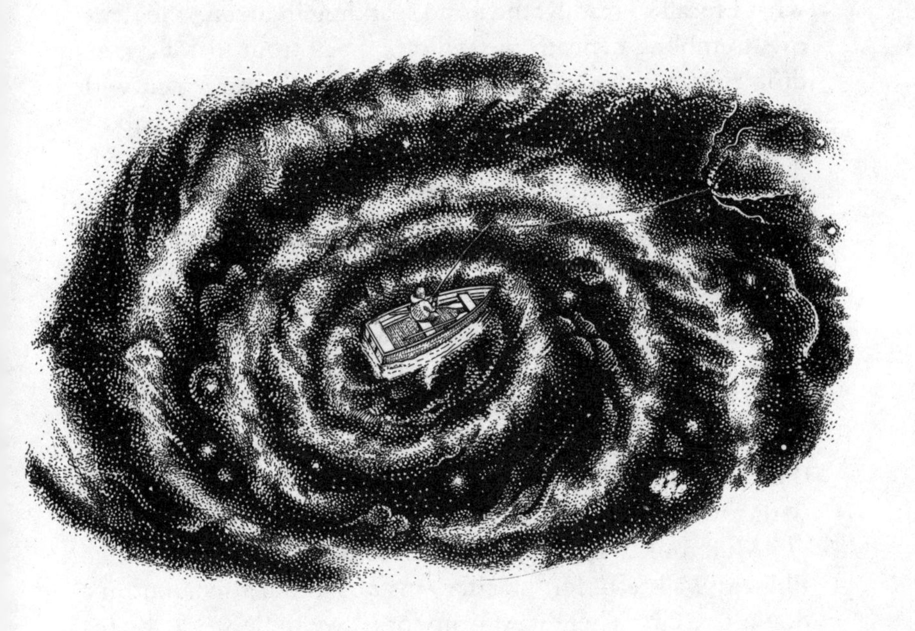

MILL BROOK FLOWED COLD AND THE COLOR OF ICED TEA from the cedar swamp at the top of the property. At one time there were trout-rearing ponds there, but they were abandoned so long ago that before I was born the concrete forms had filled with moss and cedar trees and decay. When I was a child I sometimes visited the swamp, but there was something unpleasant about the place. It seemed haunted. I preferred to be downstream at Millbrook Pond, where the lawn sloped to the shore in open sunshine, where life was lived in the present.

My brother will not remember this fondly, if he remembers it at all. He was seventeen that summer, perhaps already past the age when events carry the significance that makes memories of childhood so vivid. I doubt if he remembers what I recall so readily: the pond sparkling in breeze, the shadows trembling beneath the willows, small trout making raindrop rings on the surface. The old dam was overgrown with grasses and ivy that hung from its edge like eyelids, and above it was a massive iron wheel that could be turned to raise and lower the floodgate. The lawn, big as a city park, stretched up from the pond and was shaded by willows near the water and, farther up, by maples and elms and exotic flowering trees. Above the lawn was the house, fronted with white columns, capped with gables, cupolas, and baroque trim—an antebellum mansion set incongruously in northern Michigan. Past the house were a circular drive, a swimming pool, then pastures bordered by white fences and neatly trimmed hedges. Beyond the last fence was our town, a small, ordinary resort town lined with rows of ordinary, boxlike houses.

Millbrook was owned by a middle-aged attorney named Phineas Wallstead. His practice was not in our town, but in a downstate city where it was run, or so we understood, by junior partners and associates. As far as my friends and I could tell, Mr. Wallstead did nothing more important with his time than limp around his property inspecting the work of gardeners and handymen. He sometimes spent an hour standing on the shore of his pond making long, faultless casts with a bamboo fly rod.

Though I was a frequent visitor to Millbrook, invited several times each summer to picnics and birthday parties, I am sure the old lawyer spoke to me only once, on a bright afternoon when I stood near the dam watching the pond. The Wallstead daughters had discovered a water snake on the lawn and summoned their father from the house with their screams. He limped across the yard loading a double-barreled shotgun, followed the frantic directions of his daughters, and found and killed the snake. He slid his shotgun beneath it and lifted it in the air for examination. It was a very large snake, as big around as a man's wrist. Where the head had been it was shattered, like the exploded end of a trick cigar. He carried it to where I stood on the dam and let it slip off into the water. It sank in a slow spiral and came to rest belly-up on the bottom, white and grotesquely magnified.

The lawyer looked at me then, as if I had just come to his attention. "I've got a brown trout in there that'll eat that snake by morning," he said. "Eat's all my brook trout too. I wish somebody would catch the son of a bitch and get him out of here."

After a moment he opened his shotgun, expelling the spent shell. "I've seen the bastard," he said. "He's about three feet long."

The next day, very early in the morning, I rode my bicycle to Millbrook Pond and peered into the water near the dam. The snake was gone. Proof, I thought.

WE WERE NEIGHBORHOOD children, raised in the shadow of Millbrook, and even if it or its residents had never been mentioned (but they were, often, by all the adults and children of our town), it would have maintained a prominence in our lives. Our special game was to sneak onto the grounds, either upstream to the dam and its wet, mossy stairway, or downstream from the county road, through the swamp and past the old rearing ponds. Such stealth was an indulgence. Mrs. Wallstead always made it clear that we were welcome, at least those of us with a modicum of manners and upbringing, and she would often invite us to small parties of soft drinks and cookies on the lawn. Her daughters, most of them already adults during the time I remember, were seldom present, though the grandchildren—slender, carefully groomed children who often misbehaved—sometimes attended.

The youngest daughter, Anne, at sixteen already an adult

from my perspective, had little tolerance for her nephews and nieces and therefore won my admiration. She was a redhead, the flaming kind, with skin that burned and peeled continuously through the summer. I knew her from previous summers when she broke an unwritten code established by her sisters and chose to swim at the public beach in town rather than remain cloistered at the swimming pool at Millbrook. My brother met her there, at the beach.

That year Robert seemed to have stepped into manhood, to have become suddenly old enough to marry and go to war. He worked as a carpenter, hauling two-by-fours for a local framing contractor, and by July was lean, brown, and strong. He had the long torso and wide shoulders of an athlete, but had played no sports since he was old enough to work. On the beach on Sundays, he asserted an unintentional dominance over the summer people his age. He could never be mistaken for those others—his tan was uneven, his ankles banded in white—yet the young men who passed their summers sailing and playing tennis secretly watched him as if to judge themselves in his reflection.

One evening Robert announced to our parents that he and I had been invited to visit Millbrook to fish for trout in the pond. Nothing was said about the girl.

MOONLIGHT GLITTERED ON the pond. From the house, beyond the racket of frogs and crickets, came voices and the merry, glasslike laughter of young women. Light spilled from all the windows, downstairs and up.

Our visits had become a weekly ritual. Every Friday evening Mr. and Mrs. Wallstead went out, leaving Anne to entertain her friends at the house. Robert was there, inside the brightly lit rooms and the laughter, while I drifted alone on the pond in a wooden rowboat that needed regular bailing with a coffee can. My casts arched into darkness and ended in distant splashes. When I moved the boat, the oars dipped into moonlight, fragmenting it, lifting showers of flashing water.

I have never been so bewitched. The darkness and the black depths frightened me, but I was drawn to them, perhaps because they were the only appropriate setting for my ambitions. The pond was larger at night, richer with possibilities, and it seemed mine alone. During the day people were always about: daughters and grandchildren, well-dressed guests who stood in clusters on the lawn, bathers splashing in the pool. During the day, the few times I was invited to fish, I caught nothing but small brook trout with an ease I soon found uninteresting. When occasionally a twelve-inch brown trout swam within sight, it ignored my bait and lures with such disdain that I despaired of ever catching a truly large one. Only at night, I thought, could I hope to deceive such a trout. I knew of local anglers who occasionally caught enormous brown trout from nearby rivers after midnight, and who claimed that such trout could only be fooled with patience and stealth. I had patience—the patience of a saint or a madman—and was as stealthy as any twelve-year-old can be. But I banged gunwales in the darkness, let oar grips slip from my hands, cast lures that when they struck the water sounded like stones thrown by mischievous children. My presence invariably hushed the frogs to silence on whichever shore I was nearest.

Some nights the party spilled from the house into the yard. I remember watching two girls leave the house and wander down to the pond. I was aware of them the instant they stepped outside, outlined in the light of the open door, their shadows already stepping ahead of them across the lawn. By their manners and speech I knew they were the daughters of wealthy resorters staying in their summer homes on the lake, members of a class of people I would never infiltrate or understand. They had always been a curse to us local kids, appearing every summer to crowd our beaches and movie theater, shopping at downtown stores with their parents' credit cards, reminding us perhaps unintentionally of our shortcomings.

I sat motionless in the boat, imagining that the girls could not see me. Then one called out to ask if I had caught anything. She spoke in the same patronizing tone I often heard girls my own age use on younger children. I was suddenly ashamed to be there, as if I were an intruder, a transgressor, and I said that I had caught nothing, which was true, and that I was soon going home, which was not. But something was spoiled. After they rejoined the party I rowed to shore and sat in the shadows watching the house until Robert came down in his white shirt and led me home.

Robert seldom spoke to me those days, and when he did, asking standard questions about the fishing, he did not wait for an answer and did not hear one when I gave it. At home he closed himself in his room, refusing to come out for meals, and sometimes he stayed so long in the bathroom that the family pounded on the door in turmoil. He had been driving the family station wagon for a year, but suddenly, and for the first time, he was too old for the ten-speed bicycle that had remained his primary summer transportation. There were terrible arguments when he demanded the car for an afternoon trip to the beach or to go downtown—excursions that before had always been reserved for bicycles. When we visited Millbrook on Fridays he was allowed to use the car because of me, yet he would park it on a side street a block away from the house, and we would walk the remainder of the distance on the dark sidewalk. I carried my rod and tackle box and thought bright thoughts of trout and glory. Usually I chattered mindlessly, but even in my fever I could see that my brother was not interested.

One night I cast a spinner into the deep water near the dam and halfway back to the boat something stopped it. For a moment I experienced absolute black panic. It was as if my line had been grabbed by that malevolent hand that lurks in the caverns, pits, and black swirling rivers of children's nightmares. I set the hook—an act of pure reflex, like throwing my hand up to protect my face—and could feel the throbbing and lunging of a fish. It seemed massive and powerful, beyond my abilities. Only the thought that all the people in the house would come running kept me from bellowing in terror for Robert.

Something thrashed on the surface, suspended nearly helpless by my bent rod, and I stabbed and swooped with the landing net until it was entangled and could be thrown in the boat. I searched until I gripped the fish, killing it with my hands. For a moment it seemed huge, a monster, an eater of snakes. Even after I found the flashlight and shined it on the trout it seemed unnaturally large. But as quickly as my eyes adjusted to the light the fish dwindled to fourteen or fifteen inches long, an ordinary brown trout of unexceptional dimensions.

Still, it was a decent fish, a good fish, the largest trout I had ever caught. I looked automatically toward the house. Only one light shone in a downstairs window. There was no music or laughter. I realized that my hands were shaking and busied them unhooking the trout and untangling the treble hook from the net. It made the night larger, the house darkened and quiet like that, and I kept looking back at it for reassurance. I found reasons to keep the flashlight lit.

When Robert finally appeared on the shore, it seemed much later than usual. I wanted to ask him about the lights in the house, but before I could speak he saw the trout in the flashlight gleam. He bent close to look at it, slapped me on the back, shook my hand, looked again at the trout. He made me describe how I caught it, and in the telling I lived through a version of the story that was already subtly revised. He shook his head, saying, "Damn fine fish, excellent fish, damn near a trophy."

Each day that week, to fill the time, I fished in the creek below the dam. I caught trout, but they were small fish anyone could have caught. I knew even then it would take something uncommon to stir me deeply again. Every cast into the tiny pools and pockets of the creek, I expected to feel the pull of something powerful and wild. I wandered all day along the creek, thinking of the pond. In the evenings my parents sent Robert to find me. Often it was he who talked during the ride home, I who was silent and brooding.

Early one morning, before my parents or brother were awake, I rode my bicycle to the creek and ran upstream to the dam. In the gray light before the sun was quite up I crawled on my hands and knees through the wet grass until I could look over the edge into the depths near the spillway, where I had watched the snake spiral to the bottom. I saw something, only a glimpse, hardly more than a shadow. For a moment it seemed to float just at the edge of my vision: something enormous, ponderous, much broader and richer than I had ever considered within my reach. It was presumptuous of me to imagine it could be mine, but I had already had a taste of glory and I wanted more. I had taken one brown trout from the pond, I had been praised, all the world's possibilities seemed open to me. I went home incoherent with excitement. I closed myself in my room, avoided meals, dreamed and fumed.

THAT FRIDAY THERE were no bright lights glaring from the house, no laughter, no prep-school talk spilling into the yard. The single lamp glowed in the same downstairs window. I sat in the boat in the darkness, aware vaguely of the cool scent of mint and cedar settling down from the swamp upstream. A few inches of water had gathered in the boat, soaking my tennis shoes. My casts were aimed toward the dam. I could not see it but I knew by the sound of the lure splashing in the darkness how close I was to the concrete, where the water was deepest. I imagined the lure sinking into those depths, its blade fluttering when it was activated with the vital throbbing motion that would attract and enrage a trout.

Car lights passed overhead, scanning the tops of the trees. I heard an engine, the muffled slam of car doors. Voices emerged from the darkness. At first they were low, normal, then they grew louder until they were like the voices I often heard on Saturday nights through my open bedroom window, coming from the direction of the taverns downtown. The sound drew me away from the pond and I looked up at the house. It was lit again, nearly every window glaring brightly. The voices came from inside.

I cast, reeled as quickly as I could, then cast again toward the deep water near the spillway. I tried not to hear the voices, the way a small child tries not to hear an argument between his parents. The spinner reached bottom and I retrieved it. I cast again, imagining myself sinking with the lure into the water. I could feel the metal blade rotating around the shaft, could almost see the waves of disturbance as the lure swam throbbing through the pond. I tried by force of will to make a trout strike. Not just any trout, *the* trout, the snake eater, the three-foot son of a bitch the lawyer wanted caught and killed and taken from his pond. I wanted so badly to catch that trout that the anticipation of it made me sick to my stomach. Robert would slap me on the back until it hurt. My father would take me to the newspaper office and pound on the door until somebody opened up and took my picture and wrote down the story exactly as it happened.

For a moment, with the lure nearly to the boat, I felt a change. The boat and I became the center of the night, surrounded by space charged with what seemed like static electricity. I was so expectant, so certain that an event of importance was about to engulf me, that tremors rushed down and up my back and the hair on my forearms stood erect, electrified.

Suddenly the spinner erupted from the water and struck

sharply against the tip of my rod. I jumped as if I had been stabbed.

Robert stood on the shore of the pond. He was talking. "Do you hear me? It's time to go home."

"But it's early!" I cried. "We can't go now!"

His voice was quiet and cold. "You're done. It's time to go home."

"Robert! We can't! My trout! I haven't caught my trout!"

He seemed to be laughing. "You little idiot. There's no trout. Don't you know that? There never was a giant trout in this stinking pond."

I REMEMBER ONCE Robert saying that I, at twelve, had reached the best age and that at seventeen I would see the world much differently. I wondered if I would ever see things the same as he, or if he would always be one age ahead. Would he, in my place, still remember a trout he failed to catch, even to clearly see, twenty-five years ago? I don't know. He would not remember what I remember anyway.

Robert's life is consumed now by his work, by the construction of dams and hydroelectric plants, the harnessing of major rivers. Sometimes he calls late at night, alarming my wife and me, but always it is to talk of the frustrations and triumphs of his work, of the labor difficulties in Bogota and Aswan, the shortage of materials in Fairbanks and Khartoum. I have wanted to ask him many questions about our childhood. But it would seem so long ago, so small to him.

For years I thought of going back to Millbrook, but it is far away now, across the continent. After the old attorney died, his wife and daughters sold the house and the grounds and moved to the city. A few years later the dam became weak and unsafe and had to be dismantled.

Someday I suppose I could go back. I'm sure our town will have changed little. There will be the same divisions of class, the same small matters of concern and fascination. The taverns will still be noisy on Saturday nights, and the public beach will be filled with town kids and summer kids, all trying to live up to the imagined standards of the others.

I'm sure many people witnessed the dismantling of the dam. It would have been the big event of the summer. If I went back I know I could find someone who was there, perhaps an old friend of my parents. We would go to Millbrook and stand together beneath the willows along the old shoreline, and he would tell me what he saw as the water fell; what rested, finally, in the rich black mud on the bottom.

The Ice

THEY WERE ARGUING AGAIN. I COULD HEAR THE VOICES below in the kitchen, but not the words, until I crept to the heat register. Then I listened to them argue about Gene. The boy was still a child. Old enough to dance, old enough to pay the fiddler. He was driving their son away. How dare she say that in his own house?

And so on.

I dressed quickly in my warmest clothes, quiet not to wake the others, then sneaked down the stairs and outside and ran through the snow to the river.

Later that day Father blamed Gene for a snow shovel that was left outside and lost. Gene might not have lost it. Maybe

I did. Maybe Joey or Charles left it near the road, where the snowplow hooked it and carried it away. But Father said Gene was responsible because he was the oldest, he was nearly a man, and it was time he started pulling his weight.

"I don't know where the goddamned snow shovel is," Gene said.

"Don't talk like that in this house."

"I'll leave then."

"Maybe you'd better."

Mother said, "Gene, do what your father asks."

"He's not my father."

"Just please do what he asks."

"Well, he's not my father."

"I'm not your father, but you're sure as hell sleeping under the roof of my house and eating the food I put on the table."

"I'm leaving."

Gene slammed the door behind him, rattling the glass in all the windows. Charles and Joey and I were left to face Father ourselves. But he looked at us and said, "Don't you have chores?" and we were out the door, running for the river.

"Who lost the goddamned shovel?" Charlie asked.

"Probably Pissant here."

"Not me," I said. But I wasn't sure.

It had been a cold winter, the coldest we had ever known, and for the first time in our memories the river had frozen from bank to bank. The river was not fast, but it was large and deep and powerful enough to resist freezing. In summer, when the wind turned the surface to chop, it was difficult to notice current at all until you looked closely and saw the deep reach of it, the way it rose from the depths into silent swirls and upswells that disrupted the patterns of order imposed by the wind. Most winters ice formed only along the edges and in the sloughs and bays the current did not enter. We never imagined it would freeze entirely across.

That winter, on the hill below the house, we built a long,

winding bobsled run. We worked on it for days, packing the snow in shape with the flats of shovels, then sprinkling it with buckets of water we carried up from a hole Gene cut for us at the edge of the river. The finished track began beside the house and ended near the river in the space between the boathouses. We rode down on our bellies on runner sleds, skidding on the turns, going so fast our eyes ran with tears. Just before vaulting over the bank onto the ice, we spilled off into the loose snow and stopped.

Charles said, "You ride out on that ice, you'll cut through, sink, be drowned in about a minute."

Once I fell off my sled and it kept going and skittered onto the ice.

Joey ran up to the garage for a rope. Charles found a long stick, but it was not long enough to reach the sled. We tried to lasso it with the rope but it fell short, so Charles and Joey tied the rope around my waist and I walked out on the ice. I could feel the water flowing beneath it, like fingers dragging on the underside. It was twenty feet deep there. I imagined I was walking across the roof of a church.

"Jump up and down."

The ice did not break. "It's strong," I said.

Charles and Joey came out a foot at a time and we stood together.

Frozen, the river had changed entirely. It seemed more like a lake than a river, tapered at each end, wide across the middle to the far shore where the hills and the woods rose away. We imagined what was beneath the ice, the water darker and the current heavier and more dangerous than in summer, imagined the horror of breaking through and being sucked underneath. We retrieved the sled and hurried to shore.

WINTER WAS SOMETHING to be endured, like school. In winter Father had no work and spent much of each day in the kitchen, in Mother's way. Idleness was difficult for him. The house became very small in winter, and we learned to become very small and quiet ourselves.

In the summer, though there were many chores, we could swim, fish, and explore the river. Father was busy repairing outboard motors and renting boats to fishermen who followed the signs from the highway and parked in the dirt lot next to the house. Gene had jobs in town, but on his days off he helped Father or was hired by fishermen to guide them on the river. He knew where the biggest bass were, knew the holes where you could find schools of walleye. Charles and Joey kept the boats bailed and clean, and when there were customers, delivered live bait from the old refrigerator in the boathouse. If they were not working they cut and stacked firewood or mowed the lawn or slashed the brush that grew up every year along the riverbank. I helped Mother in the garden or played quietly by myself.

If Charles and Joey had the morning free, we tied ourselves into bulky life jackets and took one of the boats upriver, running against the current with the old Johnson outboard Father had taken in trade. We motored upstream to the abandoned docks at Pine Island, tied the boat to the pilings, and swam or fished. Sometimes we explored the island, but it was a frightening place, spoiled by blackberry thickets too dense to enter and piles of rotting lumber spiked with nails. Duck hunters had built wooden blinds along the shore. We sat in them, hidden from passing boats, and frightened ourselves with stories of ghosts and murders. Sometimes we talked about Gene's father, a sawmill laborer from Grand Ledge our mother had married long before we were born. They had lived in a small white house near the mill, and Gene had learned to ride a bicycle on the cracked narrow sidewalks of the neighborhood, had made friendships he continued to honor long after Mother remarried and she and Gene moved to Father's house, our house, in the country. Even after hearing the story all my life, I could not imagine Mother married to someone else. With effort I visualized a tall, faceless man, taller and leaner than our own father. He was killed when a ripping blade at the sawmill exploded and fired shanks of steel through the building. A piece struck his skull and shattered it, we imagined, like porcelain.

When we became hungry we prowled the shore of the island, picking blackberries if they were ripe, searching for apples washed up on the gravel. Later we returned to the boat and drifted downstream, fishing and riding the slow current. We often caught pike and smallmouth bass. Sometimes we caught walleye, what Father called money fish because they were the best eating fish in the river and attracted the most customers. We never discussed it, but it was understood that a good catch of walleye could be cleaned and iced and sold to restaurants in Lansing. Once Charles hooked an enormous channel catfish that fought languidly, as if asleep, dreaming of escape. We pulled it into the boat and killed it with a club. Later Mother cut it into cubes and deep-fried it, but it tasted muddy, like the river, and nobody could eat it.

THE DAY THE ice moved I followed Father and Charles down to the shore and watched the ice creeping along the bank. The river was high. A week of thaw at the beginning of March had brought the snowmelt down from the tributaries. Now the wind had turned cold again, but the river continued to rise. It moaned and coughed like a room filled with sick people. Across the ice black lines had appeared, jagged and monumental as the boundaries of nations.

"She'll be moving good by morning," Father said. "Wind's coming up."

That evening Father's friends came to the house and stayed late talking. My brothers and I sat in the shadows of the living room, forgotten, listening to the men. They smoked cigars and drank whiskey from glasses. Sometimes I heard what was said, sometimes the words blended into pure sound and I began to doze.

"You sleeping, Buzzard?" Gene asked. I sat up and listened.

The talk was of hunting, the kind of talk that fills you with the scents and rustlings of the woods. The men were experienced and accomplished hunters, but were modest in their knowledge. They bragged only by suggestion. If Father asked one of them what success he had hunting in the Upper Peninsula that fall, the friend would say, "Fair luck," which meant he had killed a large buck, possibly two, and perhaps had killed an illegal doe for camp meals. They never admitted their successes, unless prodded, and it was understood that one of the obligations of friendship was to do the prodding.

Mother came into the room with ice in a bowl and put it on the table by the whiskey bottle. She wore her bathrobe and a pair of Father's socks. I stayed as still as possible, but Gene smoked a cigarette and made remarks while the men talked. Mother turned and looked at Charles and Joey and me, so I knew our time was up, and then she came over and took the cigarette from Gene's mouth and put it out in an ashtray. Gene looked so ashamed and sad that I felt terrible.

Father turned slowly and focused on us. "I told you boys to get off to bed."

Gene said, "No you didn't."

"Get your ass upstairs."

Gene stood and walked to the closet. He put on his coat.

"Where do you think you're going?" Father demanded. But the door had already closed.

Mother took my hand, and I let her lead me upstairs to the bedroom. When she wanted to let go I would not release her. I held tightly with both my hands until she looked at me.

"I'm never going to smoke, Mama," I said.

She smiled. She removed her hand and folded back the blanket and comforter.

"I'm not," I said.

"I know, Honey." She tucked the blankets to my chin and kissed me. "Go to sleep."

She left and I waited alone in the dark, listening to the voices downstairs and the clinking of ice in the glasses, and looking away into the darkness at the vague moving lights that come and go in your eyes at night. Charles and Joey came in and got in their beds. In a few minutes they were sleeping. Then I was alone again. I waited as long as I could for Gene, but he did not come home.

IN THE NIGHT Father threw open the door. The light switched on so suddenly it was like a loud noise, blaring, causing us to sit upright. "Get up," he said.

"What time is it?" Charles asked. We assumed it was time for school.

"Just get up."

It was cold. We struggled against the pull of sleep and warmth and dressed in our sweaters and jeans and double pairs of socks.

Then we could hear the wind and could feel the house groaning and creaking against it. The world was black through the windows, and only gradually did we realize it was the middle of the night. Branches beat against the glass.

Mother waited in the kitchen in her bathrobe, her hair down, gray and long. When she saw us she said, "He's out there already."

Joey said, "Can't we have breakfast first?"

"No. Better go help him."

We put on our coats, hats, and mittens and stepped outside.

Charles was first. He turned back immediately from the wind. Then he put his head down and pushed into the darkness. Joey and I followed.

I clung to Charles's coat. Already I was shivering. It was bitter cold, colder than any night that winter. Hard pellets of snow stung my face. The wind was so powerful it pulled my lips away from my teeth. I could see nothing but glimpses of tree trunks and the sudden, furiously whipping branches. Objects flew past.

Below us patches of snow moved vaguely on the river. We found shelter behind one of the boathouses.

"Where is he?" Charles called. Joey held my arm. We stepped around the building, into the wind again, and saw Father silhouetted against the river. He raised an ax into the air and drove it down into the ice. He raised it again and drove it down again but it made no sound. The ice was pale. We could see it dimly, through the corners of our eyes, shelving against the shore and rising as ponderously as glaciers.

We had never seen the ice like that. Our property was on a bend in the river, but the river was so wide and the bend so long that the current was not driven into our shore. Most years, floes of ice were dislodged from the sloughs upstream and drifted harmlessly past. Sometimes boys from town would ride the floes until they were far from shore and had to be rescued by men in boats. Sometimes they were not rescued. Always the water and everything in it proceeded downstream, out of sight.

But now the wind and high water drove the river straight at us. The ice veered to our shore, and once it struck land the momentum of the wind and the current kept it coming and there seemed no way to stop it.

We went to Father, and he gave us wrecking bars and the heavy iron spuds we used to cut fishing holes in the small lake across the road. He pulled us apart, to separate positions along the shore, and demonstrated how we must use the tools to stop the ice. He did it in pantomime. In the wind we could not understand his words even when he shouted at us.

The ice came slowly, pushed by a hundred miles of moving water. It butted against the raw bank, plowed slowly through it, cleaving the topsoil, then rose beyond the ground until it seemed to come straight at us. If it burrowed too deeply into the ground it stopped, but after a moment it would fold slowly, hinging on itself, until it cracked open and the new leading edge rode over the back of the old. Sometimes the shifting ice opened the river, exposing for a few minutes water black as oil, then closing it again as more ice was pushed down by the current. I raised my spud and beat at the ice, but I could not break it. When I pried beneath it, the insistent dumb weight tried to pull the tool from my hands.

I knew the boathouses would not stop the ice. If it reached the buildings they would be crushed. The boats and drums of gasoline and the workbenches and tools and the boxes filled with propellers and recoils and motor housings would be dumped over and taken by the river. The ice and the river would claim everything, would leave the beach scoured clean as bones.

The wind did not diminish and the ice came on, endlessly. As we worked, the darkness dissolved so gradually we did not notice it. In gray light the river seemed alive, the ice moving, black streaks opening for a moment then closing. Charles beat at the ice, took a step back, beat at it, took another step back. Joey stood against the boathouse, jabbing with an iron bar. He dropped the bar finally and turned away from the wind, holding his hands over his ears.

I pretended an adult fury of effort and allowed the spud to slip from my hands onto the ice. It slid downward, increasing in speed, and disappeared without noise into the black water. Father did not notice. He swung his ax over and over into the ice, standing on top of it as if to slow its progress with his weight. It carried him slowly forward. The closer it carried him to the boathouse the more frantic he became, until he and his slashing ax threatened to fly apart.

The board-and-batten siding of the boathouse warped gradually inward. It seemed for a moment to stop the ice. The entire building shuddered, then lifted from the ground the way a man does on the back of a crowd. It tilted away and rolled over, roof down. A wooden rowboat emerged from the door and was carried off over the top of the ice.

The second building stood in place and would not let itself be carried. Soundlessly, in slow motion, it folded beneath the ice.

Father swung his ax. The ice came on. The stacked boats tumbled slowly up the hill. One of them settled in the rut of our bobsled run.

Down the shore, emerging in the dim light, came Gene. Charles and Joey and I watched, huddled together now, numb with cold. He walked purposefully, like a man on his way to work, wearing his jacket and leather boots but no hat, picking his way around piles of ice. The wind blew his hair back from his face.

When he reached us he picked up Joey's spud and began chopping at the ice shelved above the ground. He worked forward, breaking ice until he was nearly to the river, then stepped up on the ice to begin chopping it from above.

Father saw him. He started to swing his ax, then stopped and looked again. He dropped the ax and strode to Gene and struck him in the face with his fist. Gene fell to one knee, then stood up. He was as tall as Father. They braced their legs on the ice and faced each other. Behind them a black streak of water opened, swelling with the deep currents. The wind threw itself across the water, and the surface exploded into patterns.

Father leaned down and swung his fist in a wide arc, striking Gene on the side of his head. Gene did not fall. He raised the iron bar high in the air, holding it with both hands together, like an ax at the top of its swing. Father looked surprised. He stumbled backward, his feet slipping on the ice.

He was an old man in dungarees and work cap, losing his balance, and I thought he would fall on his back, slide down the inclined ice, and drop into the water. He would be swept beneath the ice by the current. There would be nothing left, no waves, no hat floating on the surface, nothing but the water swelling with current and wind. The ice would close over the water. We would climb the hill to the house and tell Mother what happened. We would be expected to grieve.

But he did not fall into the river. He stumbled back a step and slipped to his knees with his arms covering his head. Gene heaved the spud away and walked off toward the house. Father stayed there, on his knees, trying to get his breath.

Charles and Joey and I waited. Nothing had changed. Soon Father would stand, and everything would be as it was. Mother would have breakfast ready in the kitchen. The stove would be warm, the windows streaming with condensation. In time, new sheds would be built. The boats would be repaired and rented to fishermen. Charles, Joey, and I would take expeditions on the river, farther and farther away until we had explored all the islands and all the communities up and down the valley, then we would move on to other rivers and other valleys, searching for places that were new and strange and safe.

Father remained on his knees. It was terrible not to love him. We turned toward the house, to the windows yellow with light and warmth. Charles went first, then Joey, then me, climbing the frozen snow to the top of the hill, not looking back.

One Angler's World

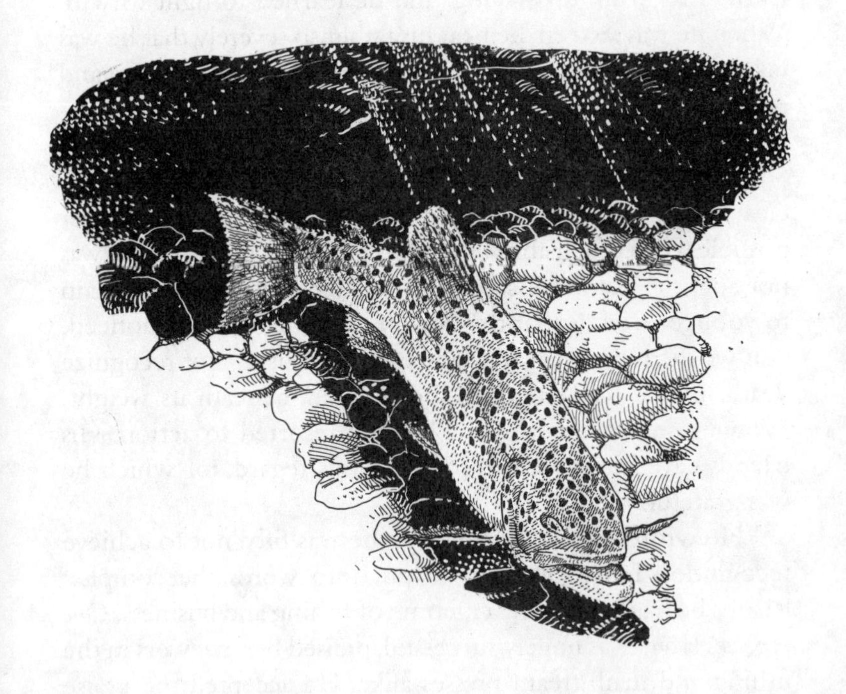

You would know him if you saw him on the river. You would know his face, lined from years of wind and sun, the eyes ice blue and distant, the abundant hair swept back and cresting like drifts of snow. You've seen his photograph in magazines, watched him on television with Curt Gowdy in Argentina and Lauren Hutton in Montana, casting fly rods with form a writer once described as "perfect as angel song." If you had the brass, and he was in a generous mood, you could approach him on the river and talk.

If he liked you he might tell you about himself. He might tell you that he had reached the age of no going back and was surprised to learn the truth about growing old. It was not what he had expected. As an adolescent he was too eager to reach the instant respectability of manhood. He took shortcuts. He learned to drink too young, and he learned to fight to win. When he was sixteen, he beat his father so severely that he was taken to the hospital in an ambulance. He left home then and never went back. He discovered he had an instinct for making money. Women adored him.

It had occurred to him that the deepest mysteries become clear only gradually, late in middle age, when it is no longer possible to do much about them. In his awkward way—he was not adept at communicating his feelings—he would explain to younger friends that the decline is too slow to be noticed, that we die by degrees so gradual most of us do not recognize death until it has us pinned, bewildered, beneath its weight. When words came hard for him he resorted to action. His friends gave him much freedom in this regard, for which he was grateful.

He wrote his first book when he was fifty, not to achieve recognition but to attempt to put into words the complex lessons he had learned in a lifetime of fishing and business. *One Angler's World* was hugely successful, praised by reviewers in the fishing and mainstream presses alike. He accepted the praise graciously, with the modesty of a man long accustomed to success. By then his businesses needed only perfunctory attention. He fished almost constantly for the next ten years.

Trout are more perceptive than we know. We rarely enter their world without their knowledge, can never blend as completely as rocks and trees, kingfishers and otters. Still, we can trust that a trout's vision is insufficient under most circumstances to detect the final few feet of a leader, a shortcoming that gives anglers some hope of success. Underwater photography reveals a leader on the surface to be indiscernible from the myriad shifting lines of current. The question is whether a trout's vision is analogous to our own, a question complicated by the enormous anatomical differences between an eye adapted to operate in a gaseous atmosphere, sending messages to an incredibly (and perhaps infinitely) complex nervous system, and one that operates in a fluid for a relatively simple nervous system centered in a brain the size of a pea.

The challenge is to remain outside the range of a trout's visual, auditory, and olfactory perceptions, and present a lifelike imitation of normal food in a discreet and believable manner. Any experienced angler is quick to argue that trout are better at evading capture than we are at capturing them. We are wise to cultivate humility.

He traveled the world fishing for salmon and trout, and everywhere he went he was welcomed as a member of the angling aristocracy. In Norway he met Deirdre, and during a week of fishing discovered that they shared many passions besides salmon. She had been raised in Boston, in a family that valued quality in all things. She had learned to fish on famous rivers in the company of famous anglers. Her education had been thorough and eclectic. She spoke French, German, and Spanish, rode horses, hunted grouse, drank and ate as heartily as a man.

She told the fisherman stories: How, when she was hardly more than a girl, a presumptuous gillie attempted to take a fly rod from her hand while she fought a ten-kilo salmon and she was so outraged that she pushed the man into the river. In her thirty-eight years she had climbed mountains on four continents, hunted big game in Africa, piloted helicopters in British Columbia, canoed alone across Labrador. She had fished everywhere, for every game fish that would take a fly.

They married shortly after returning to New York, and spent ten days in the Catskills fishing and making love with an ardor the fisherman had not known in decades. They were exactly the same height. It was her second marriage, his third. He was twenty-two years older than she.

Much amiable nonsense has been written about the habits of old trout. Brown trout, particularly, once they reach a certain size and age, take on qualities reminiscent of rogue lions. They become moody, suspicious, solitary. They indulge in cannibalism. They tend to feed at night to keep from exposing themselves to unnecessary risks but are occasionally subject to acts of self-destructive recklessness. Their effect on anglers is dramatic. Because they are thought to possess allegorical significance, they have given rise to a subgenre of angling literature, the "legendary fish" story. A legendary trout inhabits a deep, mysterious, nearly inaccessible pool, a place considered legendary in its own right, where on occasion highly skilled or naive or merely lucky anglers manage to hook and subsequently lose it. In such stories art indeed imitates life: Giant trout are seldom captured for the simple reason that they do not survive to grow large if they are careless. Never mind that in truth big trout roam considerably and do not remain long in the same pool. It is as important to believe in charmed places as it is to believe in the existence of legendary creatures. An angler who once hooks such a fish is touched with a subtle form of madness, and his days afield will never again be common. Fortunate is the man or woman who lives his days uncommonly.

The autumn after they married he suffered the first of his business setbacks. Failure was so rare in his experience that it was more a matter of curiosity than concern. A company he had built from nothing—built the way people who worked in other mediums built stone sculptures and steel skyscrapers—slipped from his possession into the possession of other men. They were men who had done nothing to deserve ownership; they were destroyers, not builders. The fisherman watched events proceed beyond his control, then waited for justice. When no justice was forthcoming he turned his back on the affair.

The fisherman and his wife decided to spend September

and October in that corner of the West where Montana, Wyoming, and Idaho come together. They leased a cabin in a grove of pines and spent their days exploring rivers and their evenings eating well and entertaining friends. After two weeks they knew every waitress and chef, every fly-shop clerk and gas-station attendant in town. They became acquainted with the tall, sallow, chain-smoking owner of a delicatessen who worked all day on a novel, his manuscript stacked beside a typewriter next to the cash register. Every morning they went to the delicatessen to buy sandwiches to be eaten later on the river. "How are the words today?" the fisherman would ask.

"The words are sluggish today," the shopkeeper would answer. "But the story has a life of its own."

One night the fisherman stayed late in a bar after dinner while Deirdre returned alone to the cabin. He sat at a noisy table, drinking bourbon and discussing fishing with a party of admirers. Eventually he was invited to join a backroom poker game presided over by a dwarf wearing a tiny tuxedo and much gold jewelry, who dealt the cards crisply and called instructions in a high, metallic voice. The fisherman took a seat and at once was at odds with a young man dressed in a white shirt with frayed French cuffs and a soiled collar. The young man fancied himself a sophisticate and was apparently powerless to resist raising every bet. On an ordinary night the fisherman could have eliminated him from the game in an hour, but that night the cards were bad, and without luck even a skilled player cannot win. He lost five hundred dollars and accused the man with the frayed cuffs of being charmless. Friends led him from the bar and drove him home. It was very late. Deirdre waited in bed, pretending to sleep.

Certain classes of artificial flies have lost (or possibly never earned) favor among serious fly fishermen. I am thinking particularly of that western standby, the Woolly Worm, certainly the crudest of all the standard patterns. Woolly Worms are tied to imitate caterpillars, it is assumed, but they are made so large and of such inexpensive materials that they can be successfully fished with a spinning rod. It is not uncommon to see off-duty ranch hands in blue jeans and cowboy boots sitting on the tailgates of their pickup trucks, backed to the edges of reservoirs, casting spinning rigs with Woolly Worms for lures. They weight their line with six or eight large splitshot crimped above the fly, and cast with gusto. Because most fishing regulations do not discriminate between types of rods, such a rig can be used on waters designated for fly-fishing only, much to the displeasure of traditional fly fishermen, who have observed that Woolly Worms are nightcrawlers in party dress and should be outlawed. Disagreements abound. Fights have broken out. Nations have gone to war.

Deirdre feared nothing. She insisted on walking alone at night, whether she was in Manhattan or in grizzly country. One evening when she was late returning to the cabin, the fisherman became frantic. The previous autumn, in a campground nearby, a man had been dragged from his tent and partially devoured by a bear. A few years earlier several women had been fatally mauled in Glacier National Park when they ventured into the backcountry while menstruating. The fisherman drove his truck up and down the five miles of road nearest the cabin, expecting any moment to see Deirdre striding defiantly in his headlights. When he did not find her he returned to the cabin to wait.

She arrived home an hour later, flushed with the cold air, oblivious to his concern. He was furious. It was past midnight. He had not called the police only because he was embarrassed. He had been afraid that if the police found her walking along the road they would laugh among themselves. They would wonder why he had allowed his wife to go out alone at night in the first place. His fury was disproportionate. She looked at him blankly, uncomprehending. He shouted at her until she wept.

I have tested dozens of rods of various designs and materials on large western rivers and the broad salmon rivers of the Atlantic Provinces and Europe, and can offer what I think is objective appraisal. Split cane, though exquisite and beautiful, is not my first choice for rigorous fishing. That opinion, admittedly, is based on fear: I would not damage what I dearly love, and I am afraid that an exquisite and frightfully expensive piece of equipment might fail while I am battling a large fish. I still prefer cane for delicate presentations of small dry flies over selective trout, but for the less subtle forms of angling—casting large flies long distances, in heavy wind, for fish of trophy dimensions—I insist on a workhorse of a rod. For years I depended on fiberglass, even in the face of derision from anglers who considered it an inferior, even gauche, material. In the last decade, however, I have converted entirely to graphite and its various composites. The reasons should be obvious. Such rods are powerful, lightweight, durable, and surprisingly (for their quality) affordable. For a few hundred dollars it is possible to purchase a splendid graphite rod that is light enough to be cast comfortably for hours, yet is powerful enough to push long lines and heavy flies into a headwind. It is interesting to note that many of the cane purists who once looked askance at my use of rods built of manmade materials have themselves hung up their bamboo in favor of graphite. My own cane rods are kept in display cases in my study. I pull them out to show to close friends, or, sometimes, for sessions of simulated fishing late at night in the living room, when I cannot sleep for dreaming of exotic adventures.

• • •

There was an early snow. It came after two weeks of sunshine and warm weather, and caught everyone off guard. The campgrounds in the area were more crowded with tourists than usual, and all day while it snowed the roads were filled with recreational vehicles escaping to lower elevations. The fisherman and his wife stayed in their cabin, reading and pacing, listening to forecasts on the radio. Because the brown trout had not yet migrated up the Madison from Hebgen Lake, they decided to wait to see what the weather would bring. If it warmed again, the river might fill with trout.

That night three fishing guides and their girlfriends showed up at the cabin on snowmobiles. They had been drinking all day, celebrating the end of the tourist season, and arrived bearing a haunch of roasted venison and a case of Bordeaux. The fisherman stood in the doorway laughing as the young men shoved one another and tumbled in the snow. Large flakes fell, streaking at angles against the pines. Light from the open door cast his shadow like an incubus across the yard.

"Get your asses inside," he shouted, and they pushed past him, stomping the snow from their boots, laughing and hooting.

The girlfriends and Deirdre sliced the venison and arranged a tray of meat and cheese. The guides opened six bottles of wine at once and passed them around. The fisherman stood in their midst, drinking from the bottles. He remained always at their center, urging conversation from them the way a conductor urges music from his orchestra.

"The fishing will get spectacular now," one of the young men said. His name was Andrew, but the fisherman always thought of him as André. It was a habit of his, bestowing secret nicknames on people. André had been educated in the East and could be pompous. With unsophisticated clients he affected a Harvard accent and dropped names. He knew the upper Madison better than anyone.

"The weather will change, and the big browns will be up from the lake by the end of the week."

"I hope you're right," the fisherman said. "These October snows have a way of continuing until May. I told Deirdre we should go to southern Idaho for the rest of the month."

"Stay here. It'll be unbelievable."

"Deirdre thinks so too."

They ate the venison and cheese and ripped hunks of French bread from loaves Deirdre had warmed in the oven. The wine made its way around. One of the guides, a tall blond who gave far too much attention to his hair (the fisherman had named him Narcissus) told an elaborate story about seducing a female client one afternoon the previous summer along the Gallatin River. The story was bold and in stunningly bad taste. While the young man talked, his girlfriend sat beside him with a sculpted smile and stared at a wall. Deirdre stood abruptly and walked into the kitchen. Narcissus seemed not to notice.

The fisherman was more observant than other people. Most people passed their days half asleep, noticing nothing but the few events that affected them directly. He noticed everything. He noticed that André was careful about what he said in the fisherman's presence because he feared that if he spoke too freely he would be revealed as a fraud. He noticed that the third guide, a handsome native Montanan named Jason "Tex" Callahan, made a point of never looking directly at Deirdre. She was so careful in reciprocating that it was clearly prearranged. The fisherman was amused. In spite of their best efforts to conceal it from the others, it was obvious that Deirdre and Tex shared a history. They seemed mixed from the same batch. The fisherman took long drinks from the wine bottles as they came to his hand. After every drink his certainty grew.

"Lovebirds," he said loudly.

Everyone went silent, waiting for him to continue. He said nothing more, and conversation resumed.

The party ended late. When the last snowmobile roared off into the night, the fisherman confronted Deirdre. She did not know what he was talking about. He made accusations. She denied them.

"You protest too loudly," he said.

"You're drunk."

"Not too drunk to see the truth."

He slept that night in a sleeping bag in his truck. In the morning he awoke cramped and sick, his mouth tasting of ashes, and for a moment he thought he was young again, waking from a joyous drunk in a strange town.

Trout and salmon landed quickly and released with care have a high rate of survival. That is to say, proper catch-and-release tactics work. In time, with the wisdom of age, I hope to apply this knowledge to human relations.

Clearly there are advantages to growing old. Experience seasons and tempers an angler. Passed through many trials by fire, he becomes hardened to the flames. He is no longer subject to most of the foolish errors of youth and is able to call upon a sizable stock of observations and lessons to meet each new challenge. If he is not educated, he is at least experienced. If he is not wise, he is at least shrewd. It is said that everyone has the face he deserves by the age of forty. By the age of sixty everyone has the soul he deserves. The astute angler, if he has lived well and paid close attention, has a soul as clean as a mountain stream.

She left early on a Friday, while the fisherman slept. In her note she insisted there was no one else. Marriage was an obsolete concept for her, she wrote, but she had remained faithful out of respect and fondness for him. She admired him and wished they could remain friends. She would never do anything to diminish him.

Saturday he drove to a few spots along the Madison but did not fish. Sunday he stayed in bed. Monday he packed his truck, closed the cabin, and drove west into Idaho. The guides had said Henry's Fork was fishing well and was very crowded with anglers. The fisherman was certain he would find old friends there.

He drove down from the high country until the snow fell behind and the sky began to break up. He turned on the radio and searched from one end of the dial to the other looking for familiar songs. Sunlight lanced the hills ahead. He would reach the river by evening and get a room in a motel and go to a restaurant where he could find friends to join him for dinner. Surely many old friends would be there. Even if he found no friends, the place was sure to be full of people, and many of them were sure to know who he was.

The Eagle Comes Down

THE OLD MAN LAY WITHOUT MOVING IN HIS RECLINER, HIS eyes closed and a blanket pulled to his chin. I wasn't sure if he was sleeping or dead. But when I stopped reading he spoke up in his quavering baritone and said, " 'An old man in a dry month, being read to by a boy, waiting for rain.' Son of a bitch."

I was that boy, sixteen years old and bored beyond endurance, reading stories out loud in August of a drought year when the river was so low the snags and jams stood out like ribs on a skeleton. The old man was waiting, not for rain, but a drink. Scotch or bourbon, it didn't matter. In an hour I would dole it out to him like medicine.

When I said nothing he opened one eye, squinted at me, and said, "T. S. Eliot. Ever hear of him?"

"Sure."

"Liar. He was a poet, American, but wished he were British. Dead now, mercifully."

"Did he fish?"

"Not a lick."

I said nothing.

"Forget him, then. Right? Is that what you're thinking?"

"I wasn't thinking nothing."

"You're heartless, Billy my boy. But then it's a heartless world."

"Why was he waiting for rain?"

"Hope, refreshment, plenitude. Many wet things denied old men."

"I wouldn't know nothing about that."

"Surprise, surprise."

Only one more hour, I thought.

"Did you know I was a poet in my youth? Until the age of twenty-five or so, when intellect, pride, and dry martinis struck me dumb. Another poet of initials, W. B. Yeats, had me well pegged some years before I was born. Listen to this:

> Why should not old men be mad?
> Some have known a likely lad
> That had a sound fly-fisher's wrist
> Turn to a drunken journalist.

"I was a likely lad, my boy. You have no idea. You think I was always shriveled up and bent over like this. But my wrist was supple as a willow. I was a wunderkind, a golden boy, the next hot thing. If you could have seen me in those days, you would have hated my guts."

"What's wrong with being a journalist?"

"A *drunken* journalist. And I wasn't even that. I was a

drunken fishing writer. I spent my life telling people how to catch fish and in the process encouraged them to go out in throngs and beat down the banks of the very rivers that were more dear to me than anything in the world. Were I a journalist I could justify the fall from poet. I could say it was like falling from Mount Olympus to a termite mound. But I fell from Olympus into a dark pit."

"It seems to me it's a lot better to write fishing books than poetry."

"It seems that way to you because you're young and don't know your ass from Adam. When I was as young and unschooled as you I had ridiculous ideas too."

Less than an hour, I thought. Maybe we could cheat the clock a little today. Maybe let him have three drinks.

"Well, your friend T.S. would be happy," I said. "It's supposed to rain tonight."

"What good's that going to do?"

"It'll bring the river up."

"Makes no difference. No trout in it anyway."

"There's enough trout."

He snorted a sort of laugh and turned away from me.

IT WAS A job. My father had gotten it for me as punishment after I was caught stealing a car one Saturday night. The car was a Rambler that belonged to my old first-grade teacher, who, I knew, always left the keys above the visor. I didn't steal it, strictly speaking, since I intended to return it early in the morning, before she awoke and after I'd used it to get to the South Branch of the Au Sable and fish through the night. But on my way back to town I ran out of gas on the highway, and a deputy appeared after I took out my fishing gear and started the long walk home. He pulled up in his patrol car and rolled along beside me at walking speed with his window down.

"What you doing, Billy?" he asked.

"Just out for a walk, Kenny. Been fishing."

"That right?"

"That's right."

"You know anything about that automobile back there? I was just wondering because it happens to be the very same model and, imagine this, the very same license number of an automobile that a Mrs. Gretel Cambridge reported stolen last night."

"I wouldn't know nothing about that," I said.

"I bet you wouldn't," he said. "Get in the car."

The deputy knew my father. He drove me home and walked me up on the porch and knocked on the screen. My father came to the door in his T-shirt and trousers, his suspenders hanging down to his knees, and stood in the doorway holding the screen open while the deputy explained what had happened.

"This time, it's nobody's business but ours," the deputy said. "Far as anybody knows we found the car out of gas with the key in the ignition and no harm done."

My father thanked him and shook his hand. We watched him walk to his patrol car, back down the driveway, and cruise silently out of sight down the street. I stepped inside, and Dad smacked me across the back of the head with his open hand and sent me to my room. The next morning, when I came down for breakfast, he told me he'd made a few telephone calls and found me a job. I was going to work for Mr. Calvin Livingstone, the fishing writer, as his personal attendant during his illness, and if I didn't do a good job my father was going to beat the hell out of me and send me to the correctional school where my two older brothers had already spent considerable time.

SO THERE I was. Personal attendant to Mr. Livingstone, who smelled of mothballs and old books and was bent and skinny and had a hooked nose and fierce eyes that made you think of a bird of prey. In his youth, his daughter later told me, his friends had actually called him the Eagle because of his nose and eyesight. But I cared nothing about that then. All I knew was that I had to sit with him for ten excruciating hours every day and listen to his lectures and read to him out of dull books and make Campbell's soup at lunch and two strong drinks at four o'clock. The days dragged on like hard time. Watching television would have been like admitting defeat, he said. He wouldn't allow it. If he was able we played cribbage or chess. Most days I read to him. After a few weeks I was convinced that I would die long before the old man did.

His health improved when the days cooled, by the end of summer. By September he was on his feet, walking short distances with a cane, first in the house, then up and down the sidewalk between the house and the garage and out onto the lawn in the hard autumn light. As soon as he was walking I tried to interest him in going fishing.

"There are no fish anymore," he said. "If you could have seen the river in the old days, you wouldn't bother with it now either."

I cared nothing about the old days, and the fishing seemed fine to me. I fished early every morning before I had to be at the old man's house and then again in the evening after his daughter came home from work and took over.

I liked his daughter a lot more than I liked him. She asked me to call her Rebecca rather than Miss Livingstone, as if she were my contemporary, not a woman old enough to be my grandmother. But she wasn't like any grandmother I had ever known. She was as tall as most men and had the strong jaw, leather face, and sun-bleached hair of a person who spends most of her time under the sky.

She owned a small horse ranch where she gave riding lessons to the daughters of the socially ambitious who had been invading our county in recent years. They were downstaters who moved north into subdivisions that had grown up among the jack pines and huckleberry bogs on the plains above the river. Some of them had built houses right on the banks, with big mowed lawns that ended at the water's edge and white fences that ran along the road and prevented trespassers from walking down through the woods to the river like we always had. I asked her if she liked those people much, and she paused and said they provided her with a living.

"So how come you're not in school?" she asked one afternoon in September, when she had just come home from the stables and was sitting on the porch in her jeans and boots, smelling of horses and drinking a Budweiser. She had on a flannel shirt and wore a red bandanna around her neck, not to look stylish but to soak up sweat.

"Dropped out," I said.

"What's your daddy say about that?"

"Nothing. Not much. But I do what I want. Besides, he dropped out himself when he was my age, so he can't complain. He's done pretty good for himself."

My father owned a body shop, the best in town, and had two or three employees and a solid reputation.

"I hear you like to fish."

"Yep."

"You good?"

"Pretty good."

"Where'd you learn?"

"My dad. Fishing the Manistee, Au Sable, and Black. We go to the Upper Peninsula every year to fish the Fox and Two Hearted and we've gone a few times to Canada and Montana."

She smiled and drank from her beer. "I learned from my dad, too," she said. "He took me to the upper Missouri when I was so little he had to hold me on his lap while I reeled in the rainbows on his fly rod. When I was older, twelve or thirteen I guess, he took me to Idaho and I fished the Big Wood River with him and Ernest Hemingway.

"Mister Hemingway tried to teach me how to box one day, and while we were messing around, I socked him right in the face and gave him a bloody nose. He laughed and laughed about that. He told everybody in the house when we went in later, and I could hear him telling the story and laughing even after I'd gone to bed and all the adults were sitting up talking and drinking. My dad was so proud I thought he was going to pop the buttons off his shirt."

"He was a good fisherman, I bet."

"My dad? The best. You've never seen anyone better. He had an instinct for it, like he knew where every fish in the river was and what they were thinking. It was natural for him to write books about it. Hell, he had no choice. He knew so much about it and loved it so much he had to write it down so he wouldn't explode."

I had little interest in books, but I knew about exploding with love for fishing. I'd quit school because I couldn't bear sitting in class in September and May when the river was so much on my mind that I could hear it whispering to me across five miles of town and farmland. Winter days, when the river was frozen over and covered with snow and looking like an unplowed road through the woods, I would get so restless and impatient that I would take my father's snowmobile and ride up and down the trails beside the river with my fly rod in its case across my lap until I found a stretch of water where the current was too strong to make ice. I'd put my rod together and cast nymphs or streamers and watch them be swept away downstream under the ice. I never caught any trout those winter days, but the activity kept me from doing something desperate.

IT WAS COLD much of September, but warm weather came back late in the month, and bugs were on the river every day. Trout fed on them as if they knew it was just a matter of weeks before the food supply disappeared and they would have to live with the lean months of winter. They swirled and slurped in the river a half mile from where I was confined in the old man's house, and there was nothing I could do about it. I tried to talk him into going fishing with me. I badgered him, insisting that he could at least walk from the road down to the riverbank and sit on a patch of grass in the sun and watch the river run by while I fished.

"Son, you're getting on my nerves."

"It'll be good for you," I said. "Get you some fresh air and sun."

"Let me tell you something. The goddamned boss of this outfit is called time. You've got quite a bit of it to waste, and I've got almost none. You give up just a little now, and I promise that in practically no time you're going to be able to fish every afternoon if you can get away with it. Now quit bothering me."

I would give him his drinks on schedule, sometimes a little early, and if I was feeling malicious I would let him have an extra shot or two. He would sleep then, and I would wander around the house, looking at his books, awards, and mementos, checking out the dozen fly rods he kept stacked in their tubes in a closet.

One day while the old man dozed, Rebecca came home early from work. She was in a foul mood. "Some bitch calls ten minutes before her three daughters are due for lessons and says she forgot what day it was. Would I mind rescheduling for tomorrow? she asks. Screw her. She's going to find my schedule is mysteriously full for the next few weeks. Anyway, I'm free for the rest of the afternoon."

"Can I go?"

"Hold on to your pants a minute. Dad says you've been pestering him to go fishing, and I happen to think it's a dandy idea. I just swung by the bridge, and there's a dozen trout rising in the hole below it. Just like you've been saying. I think we should take him down there and set him on the bank in a chair and let him cast a line over those risers. But it's going to take both of us to pull it off."

On his best days, when he was feeling strong, the old man would sometimes take a bamboo rod and go outside to practice casting on the lawn. His casts were long and confident, even in his illness, so I knew if we could get him down the steep bank to the river he'd be able to fish.

He woke up angry, as he always did, and told Rebecca it would be a frigid day in hell before he cast a fly again. But Rebecca had been dealing with him all her life, she knew her man, and she ignored his talk while she got him into a clean shirt and trousers. As she laced up his shoes he kicked at her like a child in a tantrum.

"Do that again, buster," she said, "and I'll pop you in the nose."

I got an arm around his waist and the two of us lifted him to his feet. He shook me off and walked slowly to the door.

"If we're going to go, then, dammit, let's go and get it over with."

Rebecca grabbed one of his rods and reels and a faded fishing vest bulging with fly boxes, and the three of us walked one careful step at a time out to the truck.

Outside, I saw that our luck would not hold. It had been warm for days and was humid as summer now, and the sky was growing black in the west and the clouds were getting bigger and lower. We could hear the grumble of thunder in the distance. It sounded as angry as the old man himself.

"It's gonna rain on our fool heads," he said. But he did not turn around. He stepped up into the truck on his own and slid over to the middle of the seat. Rebecca put the rod and vest in back and got behind the wheel. I sat on the other side of the old man and closed the door.

We drove the mile and a half to the bridge and pulled over on the side of the road. Three or four other vehicles were parked there, most with out-of-state license plates. The pool was a good one, but it was in the flies-only stretch, which had been publicized by magazine writers in recent years and was an automatic stop for anyone coming to fish the river. At night during the Hex hatch it could look like sale day at the shopping center. Now there were a half dozen fishermen in sight above and below the bridge, all of them casting bright fly lines with varying degrees of skill.

"This is a waste of time," Mr. Livingstone announced. "We're in the middle of a frigging Fourth of July parade. Do we have to take a number before we get in the water?" But Rebecca was stubborn, a chip off the old block, and she didn't say a word, just pulled the truck to the side of the road and got out and came around and stood by the passenger door, waited until her father slid over, and then helped him step down.

We walked him down the bank, each on a side, ignoring the fishermen watching us from the river. When we got to the bank, I realized we had forgotten a chair. We released our grip on the old man and he stood there, his thin legs spread for balance, and looked up and down the river with his mouth twisted in a look of disgust but his eyes bright. Small trout were rising in the shallows. Otherwise nothing showed. Rebecca walked up the bank to the truck and brought the rod and vest down. She slipped the vest over the old man's shoulders and put the rod together, threaded the leader and line through the guides, and handed him the rod.

He pulled a box of flies out of his vest and held it up and looked through it until he found a big, black, chewed-looking nymph. He tied it on his leader, drawing the tippet through large, exaggerated loops I knew he had to make because his eyes were bad.

The thunder was closer now, rumbling beyond the trees across the river, and the wind was swirling down the valley and lifting the surface of the water into patterns. Big drops fell, just a few at a time, but when they began to hit the water all the other fishermen starting reeling in their lines and backing out of the river. By the time they reached shore the drops were coming down harder, and the fishermen climbed the bank and got in their cars and closed the doors.

Lightning speared across the valley, but the thunder didn't sound for three or four seconds, and Rebecca said we had a few minutes. "Cast that big ugly thing out there and see what happens."

Mr. Livingstone shook line out the end of the rod, roll-cast to pull more off the reel, and false-cast a few times until he had thirty or forty feet of line in the air. He cast the nymph into the dark water just beneath the bridge and mended line immediately to keep it from dragging in the hard current.

The water was deep under the bridge, dredged out where the current funneled between the abutments. On bright days when the sun was right you could look down from the bridge and see the bottom of the pool crisscrossed with drowned logs left over from the lumber drives a hundred years ago. We all knew big trout lived there. They were sometimes hooked during the Hex hatch, but they usually dived back down into the logs and broke off. My father landed a twenty-four-inch brown there one night years ago, and I had a friend from school who caught one nearly as big with spinning gear.

While the thunderstorm swept down the valley and raindrops the size of nickels splotted around us, a fourteen-inch brown took Mr. Livingstone's nymph on the first cast and came flying out of the water like it was being chased by a predator. It flung itself around on the surface until the old man could skitter it in close to Rebecca on the bank, who trapped it in her hands and unhooked it.

The old man cast again, dropping the nymph farther up under the bridge, and hooked a trout I'm sure was bigger than the first, but he lost it before any of us saw it. He cast again and nothing happened, then cast a fourth time and hooked a seventeen-incher, a brown again, that jumped once and then fought in long, reaching lunges in all directions across the pool.

Rebecca waded into the river in her jeans and cowboy boots and waited until her father led the trout to her, then slid her hands under it, cradled it, and lifted it high for everyone to see. She unhooked it carefully and put it down gently in the shallows and swam it back and forth until it darted off on its own.

The wind bent the trees, and lightning wobbled around inside the clouds overhead. Rain came pounding across the river, but we could see that the worst of the storm was on the other side of the valley and it was passing quickly. Behind the thunderheads rolled clouds changing from black to gray and disintegrating already, with cracks of light sky showing through.

The old man never moved from his spot on the bank. He stood there with his thin white hair plastered to his skull by the rain and put another flawless cast into the river below the bridge and immediately hooked another trout that gave a series of hard, wrenching throbs deep in the pool, then ran for the fast water downstream and got off.

He reeled in, checked his leader and the point of his hook, then cast again under the bridge. He mended his line to let the nymph sink deep into the pool, and this time he hooked and fought and landed the best fish yet, a beak-nosed three-pound brown marked with yellow, brown, and red, the same colors we would be seeing in the leaves of the trees in a couple weeks.

But that was all. By the time the last trout was landed and released, the old man had had enough. He reeled in his line, and I could see his hands shaking. I reached for the rod to help him, but he pulled it away from me and cradled it in the crook of his arm. He looked over the river, downstream past the pool to the first wide riffle, then up, where the bridge made a kind of picture frame with a rectangle of river showing on the other side.

The sky was breaking up, and everything around us was growing brighter by the moment. The light made every rock and tree seem vivid and finely detailed. Looking across the river at the alders and cedars and the ranks of aspen and maple beyond, I could see more shades of green than I knew existed. The light was so striking it was like looking at the world for the first time. Every image was absolutely new and unforgettable.

Mr. Livingstone looked at Rebecca, then at me. "Don't say a thing," he said. "Not one word." He turned back to the river and stood very still for a long time. Then he gave a strong nod, and the three of us started up the bank.

The fishermen who had left the river when the rain began were waiting at the top. They had watched the old man the entire time. They stood leaning against the cars in their waders, their rods resting across the hoods of their vehicles. The old man kept his eyes on the ground as we walked up the bank and passed among the other fishermen. Somebody applauded quietly. There were whispers. They were passing his name around.

Tom Dean's Boy

TOM DEAN'S BOY WAS A TOWHEAD WITH HAIR WILD AS A palomino's mane, dressed only in cutoff jeans, and with a body so thin that even from shore you could see the outline of his ribs. He had been casting a spinning rod from the end of the dock for most of three days, since arriving at the resort with his mother and sisters. He had caught nothing.

Caroline found Wade sitting on the porch, in the shade, watching the boy. The old man was motionless in his rocking chair, an unlit cigar wedged between his fingers. He wore his khaki work clothes, but he had done no work that day. When Caroline let the screen door bang behind her he looked at her a moment, then turned back to the boy on the dock.

"Tenacious kid," he said.

"Wade, you filled him with all them stories."

"I know."

It was hot, July's worst. Visitors were amazed to learn that northern Michigan, famous for its winters, could seem tropical in summer, so hot you erupted in perspiration walking to the mailbox. At night you would lie awake on a bed stripped of everything but the undersheet, all hope of sleep gone, listening to June bugs picking at the window screens and the tireless faraway barking of somebody's chained dog.

"Talk to the boy," Caroline said.

"I've got chores to do."

"Talk to him, Wade. It ain't healthy for him to be out there alone all day."

"He fishes because it puts him closer to his daddy."

Caroline gave him one of her looks. She was a big woman. She could put a dog on its belly with that look. "It's gone too far, Wade."

The old man looked down at the cigar in his hand. It startled him to find it there, unlit. He raised it to his mouth, struck a match, and sucked the flame.

"I'll see what I can do," he said.

EMILY AND THE kids had arrived early that week, on July 1, the same as any year. Wade and Caroline had been surprised to see them. Surprised and pleased and saddened all at once. They had expected the usual slow dissolution of contact, the phone calls that ceased, the letters that became less and less frequent until finally there was nothing but a Christmas card each year, and then not even that. They would have understood. The resort, the cottage—all of it would have been too painful, too raw with memories.

After the suitcases were unpacked and the cottage was

open and alive again, Emily had come to stand on the porch of the lodge with Wade and Caroline. The girls had left for the public beach down the lake, where they could watch scrawny youths do somersaults off the diving platform. The boy had gone immediately to the dock and begun fishing. Emily stood watching him.

"He's got Tom's pole," she said.

Wade said nothing, thinking, Rod. Tom's rod.

"That's fine," Caroline said. "He should have his daddy's things."

Emily looked desperate then, hollow, her eyes big and far-off, and Wade knew exactly how she would look when she was old, his age. "I'm not sure I did the right thing coming back," she said.

Caroline stepped up to hug her. Both were crying.

"It makes you feel so strange," Emily said. "You feel like those newspaper ashes in the fireplace. So hollow and fragile. You feel like you have to keep up a good appearance, but if something happens or somebody says the wrong thing you'll just collapse in on yourself. You'll go empty and crumble into a heap of dust and ashes."

"I know, Honey," Caroline said, hugging her. "I know."

Wade had gone outside then. The boy stood at the end of the dock reeling his father's big Mitchell, standing there so skinny and unlucky it was painful to see. Wade stepped on the dock, and the boy turned and faced him for a moment with the same desperate, not-present look of his mother, his eyes wide, as if he'd seen too much of the world too soon. Then he turned back to the lake and cast again. He cast with the rod held in both hands, like a surf-caster.

"Any luck?"

He shook his head.

"I got something for you," Wade said. The boy looked at him, waiting. "It's in the shed."

"What is it?"

"You'll have to come look."

"I'm fishing."

"You can take a break."

He reeled in his lure, a small bucktail spinner, and laid the rod carefully on the dock. Wade led him to the little shed behind the boathouse where the oars, life jackets, outboard motors, and fishing tackle were stored. Wade pulled a wooden basket from beneath a stack of shelving, and from a clutter of broken starter recoils and chipped propellers lifted a metal tackle box.

"Some of these were your daddy's," he said, opening the box. Inside were trays of old lures, some rusted, some as clean as they had been the day they came from the store.

"He used to leave his favorites, in case I wanted to use them. This, for instance—" He lifted a wooden bass plug by the hooks. "This was one of his best lures. He liked to cast it for largemouths off the point in front of the island."

The lure was as big as the boy's hand. He reached for it and examined it carefully.

Wade lifted a large, battered spoon, a Daredevl. It was red with an ivory stripe marred by chips and gashes. "This was his all-time favorite. I seen him catch a twenty-two-pound northern right off that dock out front with it. It took him twenty minutes to land, a minute for every pound. He always said give him a red-and-white Daredevl, a knife, and a length of fishing line, and a man would never go hungry, except in the desert. You got a tackle box?"

"Yes, sir. It's in the cabin."

"Go get it."

The boy ran off across the lawn. Wade lifted three or four lures that had belonged to Tom and laid them on the floor. The rest were his, some as old as he was, purchased with money earned one penny at a time when he was a child. They were rich with memories now. Memories and rust. He took them out, one by one, and arranged them in rows. When the boy returned, Wade told him the stories.

He told him about fish he had seen caught off the end of the dock, northern pike so big full-grown men struggled to hold them off the ground. He let the boy look through a stack of yellow, curled photographs, and gave him a story, true or not, for each. A story too for the pike mounted over the fireplace in the lodge, a northern that had weighed just under thirty-five pounds and—this was true—had towed Wade in the rowboat nearly across the lake before he fought it close enough to gaff it. He did not mention how many years ago it had been. Now the pike's fins were chipped, and dust had turned the marble eyes milky. He had caught that pike so long ago that Wade had to make an effort to put events in order. Big changes had come to him, to the resort, to the lake. The lake was spoiled now—spoiled by too many damned fishermen and too many damned boats. The best you could hope to do now was anchor offshore and maybe catch a mess of stunted perch. Even that was a hazardous practice, what with the water-skiers and their jet-propelled speedboats.

But the boy wanted to hear stories, and Wade obliged. As he told them, it seemed to Wade that every big pike, walleye, and bass he had ever seen caught from the lake had been caught in the presence of Tom, with him holding a doubled-over rod, or waiting with a landing net or gaff hook, saying nothing, just grinning that broad, white-toothed smile of his.

"Son of a bitch, Tom," Wade would say. "That's some northern."

And Tom would stand there grinning while he admired the fish, saying, "You're right, Wade. That one's a peach."

Wade would always remember Tom Dean the way he looked when he first came to the resort, just after Korea, still in uniform: a tall, slender young man who arrived at the lodge one afternoon and paid for a cottage a month in advance. He counted out his money in ten-dollar bills, made a neat stack, and handed it to Wade. Then he looked him in the eye, grinned, and asked, "So, how's the fishing?"

They fished together every morning and evening, and even in the middle of the afternoon, when Wade had to attend to the thousand-and-one tasks he had been condemned to the day he and Caroline bought the resort, Tom Dean stood on the dock, casting. Wade decided he was the most determined angler he had ever known. He gave his full attention to it, covering methodically all the water within reach until he was convinced he had missed nothing, then moving on to the next spot and doing it again. Fishing with Tom always seemed like an event, even when they were together every day for weeks on end. It never descended to mere pastime. Each trip out—even when they would stand together on the dock casting, while the sun came up in mangled yellows and oranges over the hills across the lake—every trip, every cast held the potential for extraordinary results.

At the end of the month Tom paid for another month in advance, but he told Wade he wanted to keep busy and asked if he could help around the place. After a day and a half of working side by side reshingling cabins, Wade gave him his rent money back.

"Anybody works like you deserves a roof over his head. I should pay you wages to boot. But I won't because I know you're still gonna spend the best part of every day with that casting rod in your hand."

"That's right," Tom had said, grinning.

For the next six summers he had come alone, always for the month of July, and he and Wade fished nearly every day. In their spare time they put a new front porch on the lodge, built and painted a storage shed, a boathouse, a dock, and many benches, swings, picnic tables, and picket fences. They mowed the lawn, cultivated the garden, cut firewood, wheeled gravel from the backyard to fill the ruts that heavy rain washed from the driveway. But mostly they fished.

Some evenings they slipped off the lake early and, after cleaning and icing the fish, drove Tom's Buick to Maple City for a beer. They stepped inside the tavern, where it was so dark and cool they had to stand for a minute letting themselves catch up to it. Everybody inside knew Wade, and half of them knew Tom (even if he was summer people), and Wade would go to the bar and ask Joseph for a couple of cold ones. He would take his first long drink, and only then turn so everybody could hear, and say, "Tom Dean here just caught hisself a eighteen-pound northern."

They would have to tell the story then. Or he would, while Tom leaned against the bar grinning, and before long somebody would buy them a round, then somebody else would, and then Wade would buy one himself. In the end they would not get home until late, and Tom would walk off very carefully through the darkness to his cabin, and Wade would go off, not so carefully, to the lodge, where Caroline would be in bed pretending to sleep and dinner would be waiting wrapped in foil in the oven.

Then Tom got married and came north that year with his wife, a beautiful skinny girl named Emily, who stood eye to eye with Wade and took any hard-timing he gave her and threw it right back at him. He fell immediately in love with her. She and Caroline became friends and never minded—may not even have noticed—that the men went out on the lake and fished every day as they always had. Then the babies started coming, one every year or so, and circumstances changed a little, but Wade had been expecting that. But as the years passed other circumstances changed, more than they wanted, and it turned out that all those years Tom's heart had been ticking like a bomb set to go off. One day in January they received a telephone call from Emily informing them of a change they had never expected and could never reconcile, and suddenly everything was ruined.

So you just get old and die, Wade decided, and it doesn't matter.

Except now, after all that had happened, Emily and the kids had come for the summer. They parked their car beside their usual cottage, as if nothing had changed. And even before they were unpacked the boy had been down on the dock, casting.

THE NIGHT AFTER Wade told the boy the stories, while he and Caroline sat in their chairs reading by the light of the floor lamp, Emily came to the screen door. She knocked once and stepped inside. She was crying.

"Wade, would you come out here?" she said, already turning to go out.

Caroline was up before he was. "What is it, Emily?"

"I just need help is all."

They followed her outside. It was warm and humid; silent lightning showed on the horizon. Wade knew what was wrong before they had gone three steps. The boy was casting from the dock, there for perhaps the sixteenth consecutive hour that day. He was sorry now that he had gone on so long with the old stories. He had not realized that the boy would be so single-minded, that he would spend every spare minute on the dock, with that spinning rod in his hand, casting.

Just like his father.

Except there was a difference: The boy was squandering his days casting into a lake that was used up, dying, barren. He had been born too late, Wade figured, or in the wrong place. And now who was there to take him to the right places, to Alaska or South America or wherever it was a person had to go to find decent fishing?

Wade, Caroline, and Emily stepped carefully to the shore.

A three-quarter moon hung low in the sky. As they approached, the boy cast, and his lure landed far out in the moon's trail.

The boy spoke before they could. "Tell her," he said, not bothering to face them.

"Tell her what?" Wade asked.

"Tell her about largemouth bass."

Wade laughed in spite of himself.

"Bass feed at night, Emily. There's a chance he could get one, though I wouldn't bet the farm on it."

"He won't come in, and he hasn't eaten a thing all day."

"I'm not hungry," the boy said, still not turning.

"It's getting pretty late, son," Wade said.

"I don't care."

"It looks like your ma does, though."

The boy said nothing. Wade took Emily by the arm and led her back to shore. "I don't think you should be worried about this."

"Worried? I'm scared half to death. This has been going on for days, and it just gets worse and worse."

Wade looked at the boy. The moon's path came directly to the dock, spotlighting him there.

"I'll stay with him awhile," he said. "I could stand to do a little casting myself."

Caroline guided Emily back to the house. Wade walked to the shed and took down his old casting outfit. Attached to it was a spoon he had probably last used in Tom's company. He cut it off and returned to the beach. He had noticed the boy's tackle box at the foot of the dock.

"Mind if I borrow a plug?"

The boy turned. "Okay," he said.

Wade tied on a floating bass plug and joined the boy at the end of the dock. He stood beside him casting the lure and retrieving it so that it popped and gurgled in the water. At first he made cheerful conversation, but it was an effort. All the time, in his heart, he knew that the boy, that all of them, were being directed toward larger and more prevailing disappointments.

IN THE MORNING Wade awoke in panic. He heard cries for help and clawed himself to wakefulness like a man dreaming of drowning. All those years his secret fear had been that a child, unattended, would fall from the dock. He was up and stepping into his trousers before he was even thinking, was pushing through the screen door into the cool, gray summer dawn, noticing (but not noticing) the yellow and orange sky across the lake where the sun would be rising. He was down the steps before he saw the boy, saw the rod bent double, saw the frail, spindlelike legs spread and braced on the dock, saw the huge, swirling, roiling disturbance in the water. For a moment he was so confused that he thought he was watching Tom himself, his arms holding the rod high in triumph, his legs braced against the power of the fish.

Then the boy cried out, and Wade was running toward the shed behind the boathouse, flinging open the door, grabbing the rusty gaff from its nail and running across the beach toward the dock, not even aware that he had no shoes or shirt on.

He was beside the boy before he saw the pike. It hovered close to the surface, twenty feet from the dock, moving its tail just enough to stay upright and taut against the line. The boy tried to turn it toward them. He held the rod sideways, low, and walked slowly back until the massive head began to turn, the body pivoting behind. The boy drew it in until Wade could lean out and nearly reach it with the gaff.

But the pike was not ready. It turned, swirling water, and shot forward fifteen or twenty feet, causing the reel to ratchet smoothly. The pressure of the rod stopped it and brought it to the surface. The boy reeled and pumped. The fish turned slowly toward them.

Wade hefted the gaff and waited. The boy walked backward on the dock, keeping the rod low to the water. The pike came closer, its eyes and snout strangely doglike, the red-and-white lure clamped in its mouth.

Suddenly it flexed in the middle. The big ones always did that. When you thought they were beaten they found some hidden reserve, some capsule of determination you had not expected. That was when you lost them. They flexed with a depth of strength they hoarded until last, and surged through the water toward the deep water and the weed beds.

Wade reached and struck.

The water exploded. Wade lifted, but the pike was too heavy, too strong yet, lunging and twisting on the gaff. He could not lift more than half of it from the water. It was so heavy he was forced to drag it, afraid every moment it would wrench free. He towed it through the water the length of the dock then leaped to shore and heaved it onto the dry beach. It pounded the ground, coating itself with sand.

The boy looked at the fish, looked at Wade, looked at the fish again.

Wade could think of nothing to say. He had not seen a fish like it in years, had not believed one existed. He hardly believed it now.

The rod fell from the boy's fingers, and he ran into Wade's arms. Wade lifted him and swung him off the ground. He spun him in a circle and held him so close he could feel the boy's ribs against his own. Then he began to shout. He shouted for Caroline, for Emily, for all of them. He shouted so loud and so long he could have been shouting across the years themselves, to his parents, to Tom, calling everyone he had ever loved to come to the lake and see what this child had done.